CAT
GRAMMAR
GUIDE

Also by Linda Hart

Thesaurus of the Senses

Also by Don Hart

Anthology of Christmas Memories
Anthology of Tragedies & Triumphs

CAT GRAMMAR GUIDE

LINDA HART
DON HART

ILLUSTRATIONS AND DESIGN
BY TONYA FOREMAN

For Violet Angel Petrilla,
who joyfully loved people,
plants, and animals

Published by Four Cats Publishing LLC

Illustrations, cover, and book design by Tonya Foreman

Printed in the United States of America

ISBN: 978-0-9985529-3-4
To order additional copies, contact Four Cats Publishing LLC,
www.catgrammar.com

CONTENTS

INTRODUCTION

Grammar is not the friendliest topic. While it isn't rocket science, it can sometimes feel like a complex, secret language. There are various picky rules to follow and many ways to slip up. Grammar textbooks are often dry as dust with obscure explanations of things you should know. And if you get it wrong, other people like to point out your niggling mistakes.

In other words, grammar often lacks *fun*.

However, grammar should be more fun because it's a common game we all play together to communicate. So, if you take the humdrum subject of grammar and throw in a little ball of fur, then naturally you have a recipe for fun, even magic. In *Cat Grammar Guide*, we call in cats of all stripes (from tabbies to Turkish Vans) to help teach you practical grammar and writing advice—with a few trills and purrs included.

Why cats? First of all, why *not* cats? Cats do at least a dozen silly or charming things every day, like pounce on pillowcases or climb in a drawer or suitcase just for fun. They're curious, playful, fussy, sassy, and persistent—all good qualities for learning grammar.

Not only that, but cats, writing, and books have a long history together. Cats are known to frequent old, dusty bookstores. The older the bookstore, the more likely they have a cat to keep mice away. Libraries are also favorite hangouts for cats, where they patrol the bookshelves and take naps on sun-lit tables. Specially trained library cats (and dogs) encourage kids to read to them. And many writers have a soft spot for cats: Mark Twain, Charlotte Brontë, Ernest Hemingway, and Charles Dickens all were cat fans.

Why grammar? Well, as any cat will tell you, good grammar is like good grooming. It will help you look your best and make a good impression, especially for your writing. On the other hand, if your sentences are sloppy and bedraggled, you aren't putting your best paw (er, *foot*) forward.

So if you've been thinking about improving your writing and communication skills, or filling in missing gaps in your grammar knowledge, meow's the time to brush up on your grammar lessons and have a lot more fun doing it. Excellent grammar skills can help you build cracking good sentences and express yourself more clearly, which will enrich your life and inspire people around you.

What is this book about exactly? It's about building a strong foundation in and appreciation of English grammar—guidelines that will make you a more confident and skillful communicator. And it's about helping you rethink what grammar is and what it can do for you or for a young person in your life.

INTRODUCTION

Cat Grammar Guide is a lively reference tool for readers from middle school students to adults. It's meant to supplement a comprehensive grammar text by presenting grammar basics and highlighting solutions to common grammar trouble spots. Topics include punctuation, spelling, learning new words, subject–verb agreement, clauses, consistency, and more. With the basics covered, we'll lighten up the subject with an assortment of cat illustrations, charts, mnemonic tools, cartoons, cat puns, and poems.

Grammar Solutions

In **Section 1**, we discuss the main parts of speech, from naming nouns to reverberating verbs, along with adjectives, adverbs, pronouns, prepositions, conjunctions, and interjections. Knowing the main parts of speech well will help you construct sentences skillfully and avoid common grammar errors.

In **Section 2**, we review all manner of Pussycat Punctuation marks including periods and other powerful marks, semicolons and colons, commas (and parentheses too), apostrophes, dashes, hyphens, and quotes so you can punctuate with style.

In **Section 3**, we show how to avoid common grammar catastrophes with chapters on Possessives (or Don't Touch My Paws), Independent and Dependent Clauses ("Clawses"), Subject–Verb Agreement and Spats, and Dangling and Misplaced Modifiers (Don't Dangle These in Front of a Cat!). We also include chapters on spelling, commonly confused words, learning new words, and consistency.

Note that we were inspired to write this book because of our love of animals, especially cats, whose good nature and curiosity make life a more joyful experience. Cats were our constant companions as we worked, frequently looking over our shoulders as we wrote drafts and created the illustrations and layouts. If you have a cat or dog, you know how encouraging they can be as you're trying new things. Along the way, we were excited to learn more about cats and their

amazing qualities. We were especially intrigued by stories of ordinary cats who inspired people in extraordinary ways. For example, a black cat named Mačak sparked a young boy's lifelong fascination with electricity. The boy's name was Nikola Tesla, who later invented the alternating current system and other useful devices. As an adult, Tesla wrote about the startling impact his cat had on him as a boy:

> In the dusk of the evening as I stroked Mačak's back, I saw a miracle which made me speechless with amazement. Mačak's back was a sheet of light, and my hand produced a shower of crackling sparks loud enough to be heard all over the house...I cannot exaggerate the effect of this marvelous night on my childish imagination. Day after day I have asked myself, what is electricity?
>
> —*Tesla: Life and Legacy*, www.pbs.org

If a childhood cat can light up a boy's imagination, surely a few fuzzy friends can add a bit of sparkle to the "mundane" topic of grammar. As you take up the grand task of learning grammar in a fun, new way, we invite you to share the adventure with the furry companions in this book.

Cats | can find | center
the / of excitement
in situation.
any

THE NINE LIVES OF CATS

From their first life, we truly are smitten:
'Tis the life of the newly born kitten.

Their second life is surely a thrill.
It's the life of exploring at will.

Their third life is finding some fun
By discovering green grass, plants, and the sun.

Their fourth life is noticing girls and boys
And learning about "cat games" and toys.

Their fifth life is full of eating and sleeping
Chasing bugs and mice that are creeping.

Their sixth life is making a friend most divine
Who will feed them and love them "so very sublime."

Their seventh life requires less stress
And a great deal more sleeping, you'd guess.

Their eighth life is spent looking for a nap
In the right house, the right chair, and the right lap.

Their ninth life winds down with economy
In the style of Old Deuteronomy.

—Don Hart

SECTION 1

PARTS OF SPEECH: GRAMMAR STAR PLAYERS

1

GRAMMAR GAMES

Cats are game for grammar. You may think grammar is a dry set of language rules. But to cats, grammar is an adventure. It's an exciting game of vibrant verbs, dramatic dashes, and curious clauses. Come to think of it, cats view almost anything as a fun sport—even things you think are drudgery. Waking up in the morning is a game they like to play with you. A load of laundry is a game. So is crumpled wrapping paper, a broom, or a spoon.

If you want to make grammar an adventure too, all you have to do is think like a cat. First, be curious about grammar. Ponder things and scratch below the surface. Be willing to peer around corners and climb through cat doors to observe things. Also, be playful but persnickety about grammar rules. Practice good grammar grooming. Be fussy if you see something out of place in your own writing. Next, be persistent. Don't give up if the rules seem confusing or complicated. Practice your grammar skills with care until you have mastered them. Finally, use your grammar skills to show a bit of cat style in your writing.

PLAYING THE GRAMMAR GAME

When you want to play any game, first you have to learn the rules. The same is true for the game of grammar. Grammar is a set of rules or conventions that helps people communicate more easily and effectively. If everyone—writers and readers—uses the same rules, then the game is on.

Perhaps you're feeling a bit fuzzy about certain grammar rules. Maybe you've always been stumped by semicolons or confused by commas. This makes playing the grammar game less fun. Also, if you frequently break accepted grammar rules, your speaking and writing may suffer. Your writing may not be acceptable to a lot of people you wish to win over.

In the chapters that follow, we'll help you become more aware of which grammar rules trip you up and hurt your game. We'll begin with Parts of Speech, the stars of the Grammar Game. Knowing the parts of speech in sentences and understanding what each one can do will help you master the game of grammar.

GRAMMAR GAME LINEUP

Parts of speech are the grammar line up that will help you create amazing sentences. We will discuss the main parts of speech in detail in Chapters 2–11. While all of the parts of speech work together, nouns and verbs play starring roles. They are the foundation of a good sentence, giving it meaning and strength. The stronger your noun and verb players are, the more forceful your writing will be.

Next, pronouns act as substitutes or pinch hitters for nouns. When they stand in for nouns, pronouns can make writing smoother and less repetitive. Adjectives and adverbs support nouns and verbs, respectively, by adding a bit of style and flair to the game.

Prepositions and conjunctions tie other parts of speech players together so the whole team works smoothly. Finally, interjections boldly add theatrics and entertainment that can enliven any game.

COACHING X'S AND O'S

In later chapters, you'll be introduced to Miss Pell, your helpful grammar and spelling teacher and coach. She'll guide you so you won't <u>Misspell</u> with Miss Pell from now on. She'll also teach you how to "use your noodle" to remember grammar and spelling rules using memory tools called *mnemonics*. You'll also get friendly grammar advice from Punctsie the Punctuation Cat.

In coming chapters, cats will be your grammar cheerleaders. They will encourage you to master each part of speech and learn the rules of the grammar game. They will encourage you to have a bit of fun with language and, at the same time, write more skillfully. As your personal pep squad, cats can entertain and motivate you to succeed.

Welcome to the exciting game of grammar. Have fun and good luck! The cats are cheering you on.

2

PARTS OF SPEECH
COOL CATS, ALLEY CATS, AND FRAIDY CATS

If you like cats, you know there are many different kinds: alley cats, cool cats (too cool for school), movie star cats, barnyard cats, fraidy cats, and fat cats, to name a few. Each type of cat has similar qualities, and they tend to behave alike. For instance, fraidy cats hide under beds, whereas movie star cats like to strike a pose.

Just as different types of cats behave similarly, so too do parts of speech. Parts of speech are groups of words that act in similar ways in a sentence. If you get to know how each part of speech behaves, you can use it effectively in your writing and avoid getting scratched.

There are eight main parts of speech: *nouns, verbs, pronouns, adjectives, adverbs, conjunctions, prepositions,* and *interjections.*

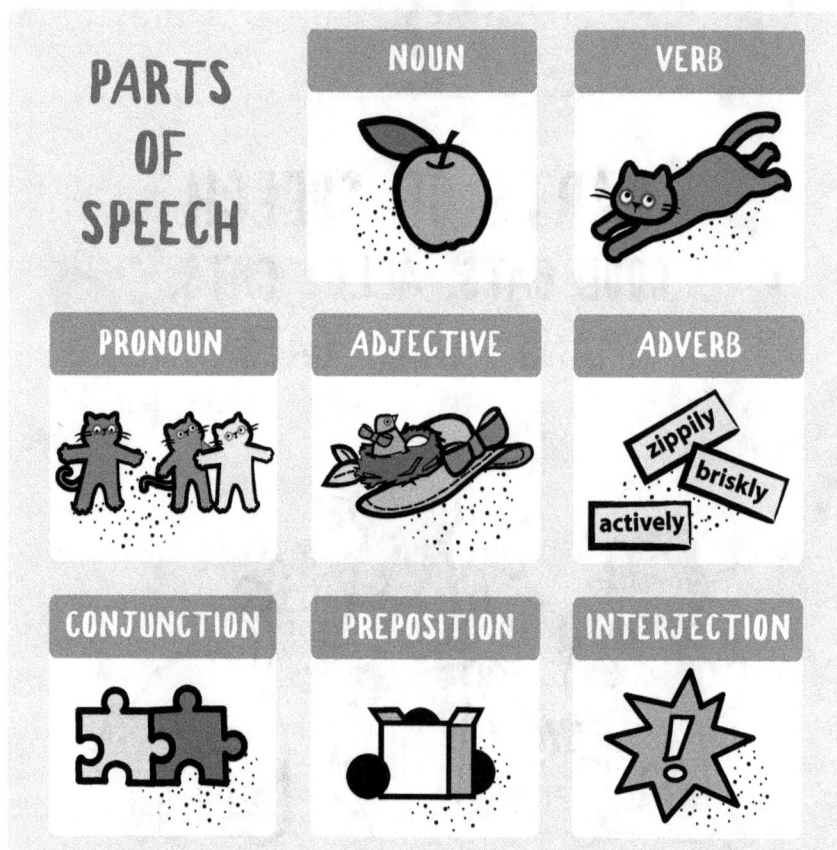

PARTS OF SPEECH

NOUN

VERB

PRONOUN

ADJECTIVE

ADVERB

zippily

briskly

actively

CONJUNCTION

PREPOSITION

INTERJECTION

Let's pause here to consider why we have different parts of speech at all. Why should we care about learning them? Parts of speech are like the cast and crew of a movie. Each one is assigned a specific role to play. Together they make the whole production come to life. Nouns and verbs are grammar stars in the spotlight. They are where the action and drama are. Without them, there is no sentence, nor story, only fragments and incomplete thoughts. The other parts of speech, such as adjectives and adverbs, play supporting roles. They make nouns and verbs really shine: making them more specific, colorful, connected, and meaningful. As the creator of your own writing, you get to select the best parts of speech for your purpose and direct them skillfully to build great sentences.

PARTS OF SPEECH: COOL CATS, ALLEY CATS, AND FRAIDY CATS

In the chapters that follow, we'll discuss the different parts of speech and see what each one can do for you. Learning the parts of speech well can help you compose all sorts of delightful and intriguing sentences. And, if you want to get really fancy, you can learn to use the more unusual parts of speech, such as *gerunds* and *participles*. If you know what these are, you'll impress your friends and amaze your fans. Cool cat!

3

NAMING NOUNS

![image]()

PLACES

PEOPLE

THINGS

Nouns are naming words. They name people and living things, places, objects, natural phenomena, ideas, qualities, and concepts. Each noun is a special name bestowed: *kitten, Serengeti, crescendo, debacle, balloon, chrysanthemum, volcano, ruby.* Of all the parts of speech, nouns may be the most captivating because they inhabit a space—either a physical space or a space within our imaginations—and there they can leave a deep mark on us.

Nouns are the doers (subjects) and receivers (direct or indirect objects) of action. They can be single words (*apple, spoon*) or groups of words (*baker's dozen*). Nouns are the *pies,* the *pie throwers,* and the *people* getting hit in the face with a pie. Nouns are the *pie ingredients*, the *pie recipes*, the *pie shops*, the *notion* of having pie for breakfast, and all manner of "pie in the sky" *ideas*. (Question: what are pies doing in the sky anyway?)

ROLES OF NOUNS

Nouns play several different roles in sentences. Like actors in a play, they can be the main part or a bit character. They can be the butt of a joke, the object of affection, or only vaguely mentioned off-stage. For good grammar, keep tabs on the nouns because they provide the drama (and sometimes the comedy) in writing.

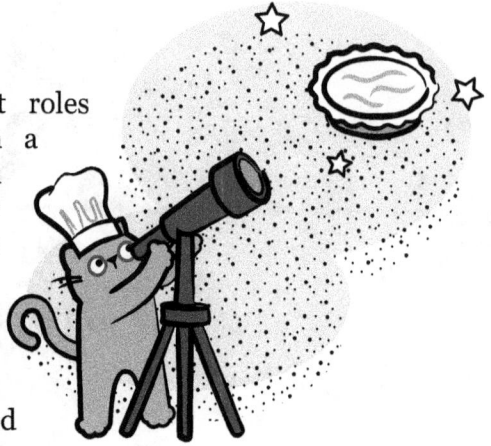

Nouns as subjects and subject complements. The most important role of a noun is as a *subject*. Subjects play the lead role in a sentence. They are the *who* and the *what* in a sentence. They act with a verb to create a complete thought.

> The <u>baker</u> ran out of flour.

In the sentence above, *baker* acts as the subject. Subjects often, but not always, appear at the beginning of a sentence. With their associated verbs, they form the core of a sentence. Subjects can be single words such as *cake* or *laughter*, several words such as *cookie cutter, puff pastry*, or *oven door*, and proper names such as *My Oh My Pie Shoppe*. Subjects can even be whole <u>phrases</u>:

> <u>Pie in the sky</u> is a fanciful wish.
>
> <u>Swirling the frosting</u> takes time.

When they are subjects, nouns like to be the Top Dog in a sentence, whereas their accompanying verbs are like a dashing cat—they're where the action is. When a subject disagrees with its verb, then you have a squabble, and things can get messy—or at least confusing for readers. So, it's better that subjects and verbs get along. For more about subject–verb agreement, see Chapter 20: Subject–Verb Agreement and Spats.

Besides subjects, nouns can function as *subject complements*. Subject complements are alternate names or stand-ins for subjects. They complement a subject by more fully describing it using a new name that follows a linking verb (*is, are, was,* etc.). For example,

Sassy is a jumper.

(*Sassy* is the subject; *jumper* is the subject complement.)

Her cherry crumble pie is a masterpiece.

(*Pie* is the subject; *masterpiece* is the subject complement because it provides another name for the pie.)

My cat Sammy is a lion in the house. Outside, he's a kitten.

(*Sammy/he* are subjects; *lion/kitten* are subject complements because they stand in for the subject.)

Nouns as objects. Nouns not only act in a sentence but also can be acted upon. If a noun is the object of an action of a verb, it is called a *direct object*. If a noun is the indirect object of a verb, it is called an *indirect object*. Indirect objects are less common because a sentence must first have a direct object to have an indirect object. Here are some examples:

Sassy leaped on the counter to get the toy mouse.
(*Counter* is the object of the preposition *on*.
Mouse is a direct object.)

Against our better judgment, we gave
<u>Sassy</u> the <u>toy</u>. (*Toy* is a direct object;
Sassy is an indirect object.)

Sassy chewed the <u>toy</u> to bits.
(*Sassy* is the subject; *toy* is a direct
object; it indicates what Sassy chewed.)

JoAnn gave <u>Jennifer</u> her secret cookie <u>recipe</u>.
(*Recipe* is the direct object; Jennifer is the indirect object.)

Violet and Andy collected <u>berries</u> for the pie.
(*Berries* is the direct object.)

I would like a slice of blueberry <u>pie</u>.
(*Pie* is the object of a preposition.)

Nouns as juggling gerunds. Some nouns look like verbs, but they are actually nouns disguised as verbs. These verb-looking nouns are called *gerunds*. Gerunds are a type of *verbal*, which are words formed from verbs but act in different ways in a sentence (such as the subject or a direct object). You could say that gerunds "juggle" the task of being a noun, even though they look like a verb.

As nouns, gerunds are often the *what* in a sentence, and they always end in "-ing." For example, the underlined words below are gerunds.

Cats enjoy <u>napping</u> more than any other activity.
(*Napping* acts as the direct object.)

<u>Sneaking</u> around the house is impossible if you are a curious giraffe. (*Sneaking* acts as the subject.)

I practiced <u>juggling</u>, while Joe played the oboe.
(*Juggling* acts as the direct object.)

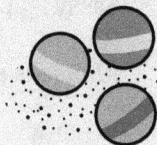

One way to remember gerunds is that they are nouns that "ing" in a sentence—*juggling, running, whistling, falling, hopping*. If you see an "ing" word, and it acts as a noun, then it's a gerund.

However, not all words that end in "-ing" are gerunds. Some "ing" words are *participles*. Participles help complete a verb or modify a noun (act as adjectives):

> The <u>napping</u> cat dreamed of bunnies and ice cream cones.
> (*Napping* modifies cat, i.e., acts as an adjective.)
>
> The parade-goers <u>were cheering</u> in a sea of confetti.
> (*Cheering* along with *were* acts as a verb.)
>
> The <u>popping</u> balloon scared the teacher.
> (*Popping* modifies balloon, i.e., acts as an adjective.)

For more about participles, see Chapter 4: Ready, Action, Verbs! For more on participles that dangle, see Chapter 21: Dangling and Misplaced Modifiers (Don't Dangle These in Front of a Cat!).

TYPES OF NOUNS

Nouns come in various types. Below are the main ones.

Common nouns are names for general people, places, and things that are abstract or concrete. Examples are *shop, counter, joy*, and *customer*.

Compound nouns have two or more words. Examples are *oven mitt, cookie sheet,* and *pie pan*.

Abstract nouns are intangible ideas, concepts, and qualities. Examples are *merriment, hunch*, and *craftsmanship*.

Gerunds are verb-looking nouns that act as subjects or objects in a sentence. Examples: *Baking* pies is an art. He likes *picking* apples.

Concrete nouns are names for tangible, specific things, such as *pan, fork, butter*, and *stove*.

Proper nouns are names for specific people, places, and things, such as *Polly's Perfect Pie Shoppe* and *Chef Jason*.

Collective nouns are names for groups of people, places, and things, such as a *bundle* of herbs, *team* of cooks, and *heap* of spices.

TYPES OF NOUNS

COMMON

Names for *general* people, places, or things

Examples: *mitten, meadow, sidewalk, bed*

COMPOUND

Two or more words to describe people, places, or things; they can be written as two separate words, joined words, or hyphenated words

Examples: *popcorn, bus stop, editor-in-chief*

ABSTRACT

Intangible ideas, concepts, feelings, actions, phenomena, and qualities

Examples: *hearsay, gratitude, bravery*

GERUND

Words formed from verbs that act as nouns in a sentence

Examples: *Gardening* is a very agreeable pastime. *Bringing* my umbrella was useless.

CONCRETE

Tangible, physical things; things that can fall on your head; things you can interact with using your five senses

Examples: *tin can, raindrop, umbrella, bowling ball, garden, bullhorn, cherry, textbook, tower, window, tree, rainbow*

PROPER

Names for *specific* people, places, or things

Examples: *Crookshanks, Tabitha Twitchit, Cheshire Manor, Cincinnati, Jupiter, Kansas, Swiss cheese, Rocky Mountain National Park*

COLLECTIVE

Nouns that describe groups of people, animals, places, or things

Examples: *flock, bouquet, galaxy, heap, pack, bundle, cluster, pair, ream, group, team*

SINGULAR VERSUS PLURAL NOUNS

Nouns come in two forms: *singular* and *plural*. A singular noun refers to one thing, person, idea, and so on. A plural noun refers to more than one thing, person, etc. For the plural form of most nouns, you add an -s or, in some cases, an -es to the end of the word. However, there are many exceptions depending on the ending letter of the noun. Also, some nouns, called irregular nouns, don't follow the normal pattern at all. Their plural forms are an altogether different word or are the same as the singular form. Here are some general rules to create plural nouns.

GENERAL RULES TO CREATE PLURAL NOUNS

RULE	EXAMPLES
For most nouns, add an -s at the end of the word to form the plural	*marshmallow – marshmallows* *boulder – boulders* *hissy fit – hissy fits*
For nouns that end with -s, -ss, -sh, -ch, -x, or -z, add -es to the end (note: in some cases, an extra s is needed before the -es)	*bunch – bunches* *wish – wishes* *box – boxes* *gas – gases*
For many nouns that end with -f or -fe, change the ending to -ves	*life – lives* *wolf – wolves* *loaf – loaves* *leaf – leaves*
However, some words ending in -f simply take an -s	*chef – chefs* *cuff – cuffs* *spoof – spoofs* *cliff – cliffs*
For nouns that end with -o, add -es or -s to the end (depending on the word)	*tomato – tomatoes* *echo – echoes* *soprano – sopranos* *shampoo – shampoos* *volcano – volcanos or volcanoes*

LEAF

LEAVES

TOMATO

TOMATOES

RULE	EXAMPLES
For nouns that end with a consonant + -y, change the ending to -ies	*puppy – puppies* *poppy – poppies* *berry – berries* *company – companies*
For nouns that end with a vowel + -y, add -s	*toy – toys* *ray – rays* *delay – delays*
For nouns that end with -us, change to -i or add -es or -ses to the end	*thesaurus – thesauri or thesauruses* *circus – circuses* *cactus – cacti or cactuses*

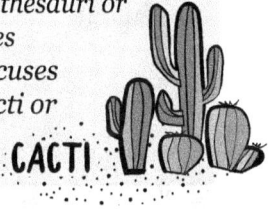

CACTUS

CACTI

RULE	EXAMPLES
For nouns that end with -is, change ending to -es	*analysis – analyses* *crisis – crises*
For nouns that end with -o preceded by a vowel, add -s	*studio – studios* *radio – radios* *zoo – zoos*
Some nouns have the same singular and plural forms	*moose – moose* *sheep – sheep* *series – series*
Some nouns have irregular plural forms that are completely different words	*goose – geese* *child – children* *mouse – mice*

GOOSE

It's important to recognize the singular and plural forms of nouns to ensure subject–verb agreement. For advice on that, see Chapter 20.

CHOOSE STRONG NOUNS

When you write, pay attention to nouns. If your nouns are vivid and strong, they can make your sentences sturdy and powerful. They are pathways of clarity for your readers. Choose nouns that paint a picture, evoke powerful emotions, or stir the senses or the imagination. Strong nouns have a presence—like a tomcat with a moustache. They're specific, colorful, and memorable. Weak nouns are vague and forgettable. A strong noun can stand on its own, without needing extra words or qualifiers to describe it. If you pair a strong noun with an active verb, your writing will pop with excitement. For example, compare the following sentences:

GOOD	BETTER
She stared at me with an angry, intense look.	Her stare shot daggers.
The cricket game was exciting and intense.	The cricket game was a barn burner.
The hefty, muscular dog walked aimlessly around the street.	The bulldog rambled through the streets.

Notice the sentences on the left are less direct and rely on adjectives or adverbs to get their point across. The ones are right are shorter and more vivid because they use strong nouns.

WHAT MAKES A STRONG NOUN?

Quality: Colorful, active, paints a picture, sensory, onomatopoeic (makes a sound)

Examples: *fortress, debacle, grandeur, parade, razor's edge, treachery, iridescence, nosedive, downpour, reservoir, stealth*

PROFOUND NOUNS

You may not have noticed, but nouns hold up the universe. Actually, ancient legends say the whole world is held up by a giant turtle, which is a noun. So there you go.

Nouns are everywhere, doing all sorts of things. Nouns are *people* and *living things* (including cats, dogs, trees, and bugs) that throb and thrive as part of this blue orb swirling in the Milky Way. Nouns are *places* near and far—places that are dear to you, like your friend's tree house or Lake Winnebago, or places you have only imagined. Nouns are *natural things* that you can hold in your hand or pop in your mouth or sniff or experience—like a downpour or the whistling wind. Nouns are all manner of *objects*, big and small—some trivial and pointless, others profound and life-giving.

A large group of nouns are abstract and hard to pin down. They are like dark matter in the night sky that you cannot see. These nouns are ideas, qualities, phenomena, notions, and concepts. Some of these nouns, like *hearsay* and *quandary*, are rather fuzzy and amorphous; others, like *treachery* and *euphoria*, are intense and visceral. Yet, they all exist in the abstract. Sometimes they show us a glimpse of themselves when they impact real things, but all of them are intangible—waiting perhaps to transform one day into something concrete.

From precious personal objects to grand ideas, nouns are indeed profound.

NOUNS TAKE CENTER STAGE

For good writing and grammar, pay attention to the nouns you use. Pick apt and powerful ones. Select nouns that are big-bellied, stern, eccentric, bold, dainty, or dapper, depending on your purpose. Name people, places, and things in your writing using vivid, specific words that readers will remember. Be a demanding director of your writing. Audition your nouns and choose ones that really shine so they stand out and eagerly speak their lines in all the roles that they play for you.

Now that you know the power of naming nouns, let's turn our attention to vibrant verbs, the foundational force of sentences.

4

READY, ACTION, VERBS!

Verbs are the spark that breathes life into nouns. They fire up writing with their energy and intensity. They *swirl, swoop, salute, pulse, rattle, contort, plummet, bark,* and *shimmy.* Verbs are the directors of action, driving the momentum of sentences. They animate nouns and pronouns to *move, feel, speak, taste, smell,* and *touch.* They also link descriptions and help other verbs. Along with nouns, verbs form the core of any sentence. If you pay attention to verbs, then you know where a sentence is going: you can see which way the cat is jumping.

Cats are all about verbs because they are often in motion—*dashing, scratching, climbing, chasing, pouncing*—or they're *sleeping,* which is also a verb, albeit a drowsy one. Cats *trill, yawn, scamper, stretch, peer,* or simply *ignore* you if they choose. In other words, cats are a bundle of life itself, just as verbs are life, captured in words.

REVVING UP THE VERBS

Imagine a sentence without any verbs. Actually, this would not be a sentence at all. It would just be a puddle of words on the page. But throw in a verb, and Boom, you've got life, drama, Action!

Verbs are words for action or states of being in a sentence. Some verbs are zippy and dramatic. They *swerve, curve, careen, crash, flutter, flap,* and *fizz.* Other verbs are subtle or internal. They *unfold, ponder, realize, revel, bask,* and *intrigue.* These verbs show what people or things are, think, or feel. Other verbs are linking or helping verbs that work with other verbs to express identity, existence, or relationship to time.

Nouns and verbs are essential for a complete sentence. A verb forms a predicate (aka predi-cat!), which is a verb plus any accompanying words, that tells us something about a subject (a noun or pronoun)— what it's doing, for instance.

Tutu the cat pushed items off the dresser to wake up George.
(*Tutu the cat* is the subject; *pushed items off the dresser to wake up George* is the predicate that contains the verbs *pushed* and *wake*.)

That calliope sounds badly out of tune.
(*Calliope* is the subject; *sounds badly out of tune* is the predicate that contains the verb *sounds*.)

Sometimes, a verb alone can make a complete sentence by itself, as in the following sentences:

Wait!

Look!

Hurry!

Actually, the sentences above contain a silent, implied "you" that acts as the subject, as in

(You) Wait!

(You) Look!

(You) Hurry!

However, you probably didn't notice the "You" because it's written in tiny mouse print. In any case, you can see how powerful verbs can be if they can carry a whole sentence by themselves. Note that verbs can have even more punch and style when they are followed by exclamation points (Help!) or question marks (See?).

TYPES OF VERBS: THEY ACT, LINK, AND HELP WHEN THEY CAN

Action verbs, also called dynamic verbs, are the most powerful type of verb. They express a physical or mental action or process. They show what a subject (a noun or pronoun) does, will do, or has done, as a physical movement, a thought, or a process. Strong, specific action verbs enliven writing. Like superheroes, action verbs can propel sentences forward with their power and pizzazz. By enlisting the five senses with action verbs, you can enrich, color, and spice up your sentences. Below are some active verbs (underlined):

We <u>averted</u> a catastrophe by <u>distracting</u> the skunk.

The eager shoppers <u>stampeded</u> through the door.

Chuck <u>hauled</u> the plants to the garden.

The old car <u>rattled</u> along the streets.

To identify an action verb, look for verbs that show what something or someone *is doing, will do,* or *has done,* as either a physical movement, a thought, or a process. Here are a few more examples (verbs underlined):

Close the door or the cat will run out!

He hollered when his neighbor left without his jacket.

She mulled over why the cake flopped.

Linking verbs (also called "to be" verbs) describe or indicate a state of being about a subject (noun or pronoun). These verbs include *is, am, are, was, were, be, becomes, been, being, seems, looks, feels, tastes, smells, sounds,* and *appears.* They link a subject to words that tell something about that subject (a noun or pronoun). Notice that linking verbs are nonaction verbs that describe a sensation, emotion, quality, or opinion. Here are some examples (linking verbs are underlined):

This old furniture looks ghastly.

Julianne seems delighted with the new puppy.

We were unsure about his strange idea.

The reporter was befuddled by the news.

Helping verbs (or auxiliary verbs) assist the main verb to show action or indicate time. They include *is, am, are, was, were, be, been, being, has, have, had, do, does, did, can, could, must, may, might, will, would, shall,* and *should.* Helping verbs can provide additional meaning and even a different tone to a sentence, depending on their use. Below are some examples (verbs are underlined).

Will you speculate on who might win the dog sled race?
(*Will* and *might* assist the main verbs *speculate* and *win.*)

Cats can jump five to six times their body length.
(*Can* assists the main verb *jump.*)

I <u>may</u> <u>take</u> a hot air balloon flight tomorrow.
(*May* assists the main verb *take*.)

I <u>could</u> <u>climb</u> that tree if I had a better rope.
(*Could* helps the main verb *climb*.)

He <u>did</u> not <u>ask</u> why Millie borrowed the pitchfork.
(*Did* helps the main verb *ask*.)

TYPES OF VERBS

LINKING

"To be" verbs; link a subject to words that tell something about that subject (noun or pronoun)

Examples: *is, am, are, was, were, be, been, becomes, being, seems, looks, feels, tastes, smells*

ACTION

Express a physical or mental action or process

Examples: *lunge, undulate, ponder, adore, scamper, crackle, squeal, nudge, heave*

HELPING

Assist other verbs to show action or time and provide additional meaning

Examples: *is, am, are, was, were, be, been, being, has, have, had, do, does, did, can, could, must, may, might, will, would, should*

VERBS THAT PARTICIPATE: PARTICIPLES

Verbs have an amazing ability to act in different ways in sentences. One of their superpowers is to form *participles*. What's a participle? It comes the root word *participare* which means *to take part in*. This is also where we get the word *participate*. How do participles participate exactly? Well, participles can act as adjectives to describe nouns. At the same time, they are used in certain verb tenses.

Participles come in two varieties: *present participles* and *past participles*. Present participles indicate action occurring in the present. For most verbs, the present participle is formed by adding -ing to a verb (e.g., *growl* > *growling*). Past participles indicate action that has already occurred. For most verbs, the past participle is formed by adding -ed to a verb (e.g., *hike* > *hiked*). Note that some irregular verbs have a different past participle form altogether.

Laugh ➡ Laughing (present participle)
Laughed (past participle)

Jump ➡ Jumping (present participle)
Jumped (past participle)

As mentioned, participles can act as adjectives. In addition, as verbs, present participles are used with a helping verb (*is, am, are*, etc.) to form the continuous tense. Past participles are used with helping verbs (*has, had, will have*) in the perfect tenses. For example,

We <u>are</u> <u>building</u> an igloo.
(*Are building* is the present participle form of the verb *build*.)

The <u>crouching</u> trees look spooky.
(*Crouching* modifies *tree*;
it acts as an adjective.)

The <u>scorching</u> heat made his throat dry.
(*Scorching* modifies *heat*; it acts as an adjective.)

He <u>had forgotten</u> to close the window. (*Had forgotten* is the past participle form of the irregular verb *forget*.)

Alexis liked the <u>tarnished</u> look of the old brass fixture. (*Tarnished* acts as an adjective.)

That <u>baked</u> pot pie smells delicious. (*Baked* modifies pie; it acts as an adjective.)

Participle phrases are groups of words containing participles that act as adjectives. For instance,

Enjoying the balmy weather, Jim leisurely played golf.

Lugging the heavy backpack uphill, Michael wished he had not packed so much.

Participle phrases should be placed near the nouns they modify so the meaning is clear (as shown above); otherwise, they may become dangling participles (see Chapter 21 for more advice).

VERBS CAN BE TENSE OR LAID BACK

Verbs are the most dynamic part of speech. They change form (are *conjugated*) based on tense (time), person, number, voice, and mood. In this sense, verbs are time travelers and shape-shifters. Their changeable nature makes them more challenging to use and master. However, verbs are also the most exciting for writing because of their power and complexity.

Verbs can appear in the present, past, and future tenses to indicate their relationship to time. Each of these tenses can be further divided into four categories: *simple, continuous, perfect*, and *perfect continuous*. If you're counting, that makes 12 different verb tenses in English! Let's take a closer look at them.

TYPES OF VERB TENSES

PRESENT TENSES

Simple Present
My cat *naps* every day.

Present Continuous
My cat *is napping* in the sun.

Present Perfect
My cat *has napped* in that spot many times.

Present Perfect Continuous
My cat *has been napping* since this afternoon.

PAST TENSES

Simple Past
Yesterday, my cat *napped* on my lap.

Past Continuous
My cat *was napping* on my lap this morning.

Past Perfect
My cat *had napped* in many different spots yesterday.

Past Perfect Continuous
My cat *had been napping* for at least an hour.

FUTURE TENSES

Simple Future
My cat *will nap* tomorrow.

Future Continuous
My cat *will be napping* soon.

Future Perfect
My cat *will have napped* in at least five different spots by the end of the week.

Future Perfect Continuous
My cat *will have been napping* for over an hour before dinner.

You'll notice from the chart above that the *simple forms* of each of the verb tenses are straightforward: they describe an action occurring right now or regularly (present tense), an action that has already occurred (past tense), or an action that will occur (future tense). Simple tenses are indeed simple and direct.

That stinks.	The tiger roared.	Will they listen?
(present)	(past)	(future)

But what about the *continuous, perfect*, and *perfect continuous* verb tenses? These terms sound like good descriptions for waterfalls or summer days, but they also are the names of verb tenses that describe more complex actions and relationships to time. The *continuous* tense uses a "to be" verb (*is, was, were,* etc.) plus a verb ending in -ing (a participle). The continuous tense indicates an ongoing action in the present, past, or future:

Tashi is snacking.   They were applauding.   I will be flying a kite.

(present continuous)   (past continuous)   (future continuous)

The *perfect* forms indicate an action or process that has been completed, or in other words, one that has been "perfected." They use the helping verbs *has/have* or *had* plus the past participle form of the verb.

I <u>have</u> <u>seen</u> that silly movie already. (present perfect)

We <u>had</u> just <u>reached</u> the entrance when the storm hit. (past perfect)

She <u>will</u> <u>have</u> <u>completed</u> her parachuting trip by tomorrow. (future perfect)

The *perfect* and *continuous* forms can be used together in the *perfect continuous* form—a lengthier, but still useful, tense.

He <u>has</u> <u>been</u> <u>yodeling</u> for two hours. (present perfect continuous)

He <u>had</u> <u>been</u> <u>yodeling</u> for two hours. (past perfect continuous)

He <u>will</u> <u>have</u> <u>been</u> <u>yodeling</u> for two hours. (future perfect continuous)

37

Each of these verb tenses brings a certain style and tone to writing. Simple tenses are more direct and straightforward. Continuous tenses carry momentum for an unfolding situation. For example, these tenses may work better when describing a suspenseful story as an eyewitness as it's happening. Perfect and perfect continuous tenses lend a certain complexity and formality to writing. These tenses can be used effectively to indicate exact time relationships. However, these tenses can sometimes be unnecessarily wordy or contorted. See what sounds best to your ear. As a writer, you get to choose verb tenses that best fit the style and tone you want to convey.

CONJUGATION CONSULTATION

Correct verb tenses also depend on verb *conjugation* or changes in verb forms depending on the tense (also called *verb inflection*). When they are conjugated according to tense, verbs can be *regular* (follow a standard pattern) or *irregular* (do not follow a standard pattern).

Regular verbs use -ed to form the past and perfect tenses. Most verbs in English are the regular kind.

EXAMPLES OF REGULAR VERBS

Present	Past	Past Participle (for perfect tenses)
jump	jumped	jumped
shout	shouted	shouted
twirl	twirled	twirled
nap	napped	napped
toss	tossed	tossed

Unlike regular verbs, irregular verbs take entirely different, nonstandard forms for past and perfect tenses. These irregular forms have no particular pattern, so it's best to memorize them and develop a good ear for how they sound when used correctly (you can find a list of all the main ones in a grammar textbook or website).

EXAMPLES OF IRREGULAR VERBS

Present	Past	Past Participle (for perfect tenses)
swim	swam	swum
bite	bit	bitten
go	went	gone
sing	sang	sung
show	showed	shown

Here are some examples of irregular verb forms:

The paper airplanes fly. (present)

The paper airplanes flew to the ground. (past)

The paper airplanes have flown away. (present perfect)

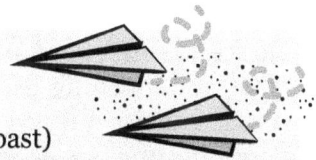

We ride our tandem bike on Saturdays. (present)

We rode our tandem bike to the farmer's market. (past)

We have ridden our tandem bike over 20 miles. (present perfect)

COMMON VERB TENSE PROBLEMS

Verb tenses are an important aspect of grammar. They can help readers understand various time relationships. With practice, you can master correct verb tenses and know which forms will sound best in your writing. However, even if you're confident and not at all tense about verb tenses, you may want to review a few common verb tense problems and see how to correct them.

Inconsistent verb tenses. Switching from one verb tense to another is confusing to readers. It makes your writing appear unsettled in terms of time and without a logical sequence of events.

> **Inconsistent**: As Penny mops the floor, her cat scampered into the kitchen.
>
> **Consistent**: As Penny mops the floor, her cat scampers into the kitchen.
>
> **Consistent**: As Penny mopped the floor, her cat scampered into the kitchen.

Notice the first example is a bit confusing because we don't know what is happening exactly. Did the cat scamper into the kitchen (possibly with muddy paws) before or after Penny mopped the floor? It's unclear, so it's best to choose one tense and stick with it. Be consistent in your writing. Decide ahead of time which tense will work best for your particular piece of writing and use it throughout your work.

Irregular verb problems. Irregular verbs are tricky because they don't follow the standard pattern (that is, add -ed to the end of the verb) to create the past and perfect tenses. English has only about 200 commonly used irregular verbs. However, irregular verbs are used much more often than regular verbs in everyday speech and writing. So, it's important to be aware of these irregular verbs and use the correct form depending on the verb tense. Otherwise, you'll strike a sour note with discerning readers. Below are some of the particularly tricky irregular verb forms.

TIP: Irregular verbs are best memorized as lists of triplets of present, past, and past participle forms (e.g., *"stink, stank, stunk"* and *"rise, rose, risen"*). Listen to the music of how each triplet sounds so you can recall it later. You might have to look up some of the more unusual ones (e.g., *"slink, slunk, slunk"* and *"forbid, forbade, forbidden"*) when you need them.

TRICKY IRREGULAR VERB TENSES

Present	Past	Past Participle (for perfect tenses)
become	became	become
eat	ate	eaten
drink	drank	drunk
go	went	gone
lie (to recline)	lay	lain
lay (to place)	laid	laid
see	saw	seen

As we discussed earlier, the perfect tense is used to indicate an action or process that has been completed already. It uses the helping verbs *has/have* or *had* (or a contraction for *has, had,* or *have*) plus the past participle form of the verb. A common mix-up with irregular verbs is to incorrectly use the *past* form instead of the *past participle* form when forming perfect tenses. For example,

Incorrect	Correct
I <u>had</u> mistakenly <u>ate</u> a dog treat.	I <u>had</u> mistakenly <u>eaten</u> a dog treat.
<u>I'd</u> mistakenly <u>ate</u> a dog treat.	<u>I'd</u> mistakenly <u>eaten</u> a dog treat.
We <u>have took</u> that road before.	We <u>have taken</u> that road before.
<u>We've took</u> that road before.	<u>We've taken</u> that road before.

Notice that the incorrect sentences on the left use the past tense form of the verb (*ate, took*) rather than the past participle form (*eaten, taken*). This is grammatically incorrect. The past participle

form, not the past form, is needed because these sentences are written in the perfect tense.

The special case of lie versus lay. The irregular verbs lie and lay can be particularly problematic. Which to form use? *Lie, lay, lain? Lay, laid?* Even cats get confused by this and want to take a nap. Let's try to straighten things out.

A cat named Punctsie lies down to sleep. When we say Punctsie *lies down*, we mean she *reclines*. Remember the "i" in *lies* and *reclines*. This will help you remember lie means to recline. This is what Punctsie is doing in the present tense. When we talk about what she did in the past and want to convey that she reclined in the past, we use *lay*.

> Punctsie *lay* in the sun all morning.
> (*Lay* is the past tense of *lie*, to recline.)

Sometimes you want to write about what has happened already or is completed, using the perfect tense. Then you would say,

> Punctsie and her kittens *have lain* on the porch every morning.

Punctsie also *lays* her kittens in the sun. This means she *places* them in the sun in the present tense. Remember the "a" in *lay* and *place*. To indicate she placed something in the past, use *laid*.

> Punctsie *laid* her kittens in the sun to keep
> them warm. (*Laid* is past tense of lay, *to place*.)

Using the perfect tense, you would say,

> Punctsie *had laid* her kittens in the sun to keep them warm.

LIE VS LAY TENSES

LIE (TO RECLINE)

She *lies* in the sun every day.
(present)

LAY (TO RECLINE)

She *lay* in the
sun yesterday.
(past)

LAIN (TO RECLINE)

She *has lain* in the
sun many times.
(present perfect)

LAY (TO PLACE)

She *lays* her kitten on the bed.
(present)

LAID (TO PLACE)

She *laid* her kitten
on the bed yesterday.
(past)

LAID (TO PLACE)

She *has laid* her kitten
on the bed many times.
(present perfect)

Awkward use of continuous verb tenses. The continuous verb tense (which uses the -ing forms of verbs) can be used effectively in writing to convey drama and an unfolding situation. However, it can also produce awkward and more wordy sentences in some cases. Consider the following examples:

My cat <u>drags</u> all of his toys downstairs and <u>puts</u> them at my feet. (simple present tense)

My cat <u>is</u> <u>dragging</u> all of his toys downstairs and <u>putting</u> them at my feet. (present continuous tense)

My cat <u>dragged</u> all of his toys downstairs and <u>put</u> them at my feet. (simple past tense)

A white streak <u>appears</u> in the sky. (simple present tense)

A white streak <u>is</u> <u>appearing</u> in the sky. (present continuous tense)

A white streak <u>appeared</u> in the sky.
(simple past tense)

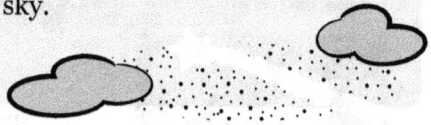

Notice the different tone and style each verb tense conveys. See which verb tense works best for your situation and for the story and tone you want to convey. Use the simple present or simple past tense if it makes your sentences stronger. By all means use the continuous verb tense if it sounds good to you. Remember to be consistent with whatever tense you decide to use.

VERB POWER

As you can see, verbs have a lot going on. They are the seat of action in any sentence. Not only that, but they can shape-shift into many forms to show tense and convey a

particular tone. Although verbs can be tricky and more complex than other parts of speech, knowing verbs well will help you master grammar and empower your writing. One key to strengthen your writing is to use active, sensory verbs. In the next chapter, we'll show you how to embolden your verbs so they captivate, electrify, and delight readers.

5

REVERBERATIONS
EMPOWERING VERBS

Ringing notes of a guitar. A roaring crowd. Driving drum beats. Sounds reverberate throughout the space, building excitement and energy all around.

To reverberate means to echo and resound. That's what powerful verbs can do too. They can rumble and boom, propelling sentences forward. At the same time, their pulsating energy lingers, striking an impression in readers' minds.

To empower your writing, empower your verbs. Choose vivid, active, strong verbs. What is a strong verb? It's one that's daring and bold.

It bounces and vibrates on the page. You can hear it clearly, and it causes a stir. You can feel its power.

So, listen to how each verb sounds in your sentences. See that they enliven your writing with their strength and vitality. Let their energy reverberate. Like a musician, choose powerful verbs to strike the notes you want, to thrill and excite your audience.

ACTIVATE VERBS WITH ACTIVE RATHER THAN PASSIVE VOICE

Verbs can be used in the active or passive form (or voice). In the active voice, the subject (a noun or pronoun) is actively doing something. In passive voice, the subject is having an action done to it by someone or something. In this sense, active voice is more dynamic than passive voice. Active voice pounces. Passive voice watches from the window and yawns. Let's see some examples.

Active voice: The kids read their favorite comic books.

Cats love sardines.

Chloe played the tuba.

An eager poodle rang my doorbell.

Passive voice: The favorite comic books were read by the kids.

Sardines are loved by cats.

The tuba was played by Chloe.

My doorbell was rung by an eager poodle.

As you can see, active voice is direct, clear, and in many cases more vivid than passive voice. Active voice "tells it like it is." It pops and zings. Passive voice, on the other hand, is less direct. It focuses on the object of the action rather than on the subject doing the action. In other words, it somewhat obscures the *doer* of the action. For this reason, passive voice is often more clunky and awkward sounding. Let's see another example:

Passive voice: The Christmas tree was knocked over by the cat.

Active voice: The cat knocked over the Christmas tree.

Hyperactive: The cat lunged off the piano, crashed onto the presents, and knocked over the Christmas tree.

Notice the first sentence above using passive voice is not as strong because it misses the real action by focusing on the tree getting passively knocked over. The cat is secondary and appears at the end of the sentence. The second sentence using active voice is stronger because the action is direct—it is clear the cat knocked over the tree and is in the thick of the action. In the third sentence, it is obvious that a hyper cat has been cooped up inside and is actively investigating why a large tree (aka climbing post) is suddenly in the living room.

PASSIVE VOICE

ACTIVE VOICE

Passive voice is easy to spot in a sentence because it often uses a helping verb such as *is, was,* or *were* plus a past participle and preposition (such as *by*), for instance, "was played by" or "were read by" in the previously mentioned examples. If you're not paying attention to proactively use action verbs in your writing, it's easy to passively fall into using passive voice. Passive voice can deflate the action in writing, making it more wordy, convoluted, and impersonal. For that reason, it's usually best to favor active voice over passive voice in your writing.

However, passive voice is acceptable in some instances, such as when the doer (actor) in a sentence isn't the main focus or is unknown, or when the tone or lilt of the sentence just sounds better—softer and more tactful, for instance—using passive voice. For instance,

> Our beloved ornament was shattered to bits.
> (The focus is on the *beloved ornament*; what or who shattered it is unclear, though perhaps the cat had something to do with it!)
>
> Cats are coveted because of their cuteness.
> (Passive voice is used here but to good effect.)

However, as a general rule, be active, not passive, when expressing yourself in writing.

USE STRONG, ACTIVE VERBS THAT ENGAGE THE SENSES

If you want your writing to captivate readers, use strong action verbs. Strong verbs are energetic and vivid. They are lively and juicy and entice readers through the five senses. They convey a fuller meaning to readers because they are specific and distinctive.

Consider the verb *walk*. The word *walk* is a relatively vague word to describe a common movement. Let's see if we can liven things up and describe the motion more specifically and dynamically. How about *meander, stroll, shuffle, mosey, march,* or *scurry*? See how these more specific action verbs are fuller and more descriptive and paint a more colorful picture of the motion?

Choose your verbs carefully so they accurately and vividly describe what you're trying to say. As you write, ask yourself: am I directing each sentence boldly and clearly using descriptive, active verbs? Are the verbs I'm choosing vibrant and ready to pounce? Or are they sleepy and want to take a nap? If you notice the verbs you're using are flabby, lazy, or just plain boring, see if you can substitute more vivid, jauntier action verbs in their place. For even more impact, pair strong verbs with strong nouns. Use a thesaurus or dictionary to find the best words.

WHAT MAKES A STRONG VERB?

Quality: active, specific, sensory, visual, vivid, makes a sound, kinetic, forceful, direct (not disguised as a noun)

Examples: *claw, cackle, roar, shimmer, billow, warble, ignite, contort, whistle, slather, rumble, gobble, flinch, swoon, stampede*

An effective way to find strong verbs is to enlist your five senses to give your writing vibrancy and bounce. Sensory words light up your senses. "See" verbs bring vivid images to mind. "Hear" verbs use *onomatopoeia*. They make a satisfying sound, a sound that resembles what they describe. Touch verbs make you feel something. Smell words stir up distinct scents and odors, while taste words conjure up flavor and mouthfeel sensations.

SENSORY VERBS

SEE

glisten, flicker, tower, cascade, undulate, spiral, gleam, dazzle, plunge, swarm, glow, shimmer, effervesce, flare, ripple, spew, brim, sparkle, flash, billow, crumble, bubble, glimpse, swell

HEAR

clatter, bellow, rumble, screech, reverberate, jangle, roar, echo, hiss, warble, splutter, cackle, clang, erupt, drone, clash, trickle, croon, snap, snarl, splash, trill, whir, thrash, bark, rustle

TOUCH / MOVEMENT

contort, luxuriate, shudder, stun, sculpt, convulse, ruffle, slather, quaver, scurry, snare, jolt, collide, inflame, flinch, beckon, swoon, bristle, grimace, enthrall, puncture, transfix

SMELL

whiff, sniff, snuff, snort, reek, stink, sting, smoke, fume, puff, perfume, inhale, infuse, permeate, diffuse, scent, snuffle, steam, inhale

TASTE

salivate, gnaw, slurp, chomp, burp, quench, intoxicate, guzzle, gnash, gobble, drool, pucker, nibble, crave, crunch, devour, gag, gorge, grind, gulp, lick, bite, savor

AVOID "NOUNIFYING" VERBS

Verbs want to act and move. Sometimes, a perfectly strong verb is saddled into a being noun instead. In other words, it gets "nounified," which is like trying to run with sandbags tied around your feet. For example, compare the following sentences:

"NOUNIFIED" VERB	DIRECT VERB
She conducted an investigation.	She investigated.
They took into consideration his offer.	They considered his offer.
They were in agreement.	They agreed.
An unusual discovery was made.	We discovered something unusual.

Tiger had an observation. ← nounified

Tiger observed. ← less wordy

When a verb is "nounified," it is trapped within a noun. This weighs sentences down and makes them more wordy and less powerful. On the other hand, when a verb is free and direct, the meaning is clearer and more forceful.

When you write, pay attention to wordy expressions that disguise verbs and constrain them into noun forms. Note that these sentences often use the verbs *have, had, take, took*, or *make* along with verb-looking nouns, such as those that end in *-tion, -sion*, or *-ment* (for example, *had an observation* instead of *observed*). They also frequently use passive voice instead of a clear active voice (for example, *a decision was made* instead of *decide*). Turn these wordy, dull expressions around and let the verbs flow.

EMPOWERING VERBS

1 Favor active voice.

2 Use strong, sensory verbs.

3 Avoid "nounifying" verbs.

REVERB RECAP

Verbs are an active force in writing. They drive sentences forward. Their power can resound and echo, bringing music and vibrancy to writing. If you choose your verbs thoughtfully, using active voice and sensory qualities, their impact will reverberate throughout your writing.

6

PRONOUN POWER

Pronouns are stand-ins for nouns. They can refer to a noun previously mentioned (*they, she*) or one not specifically named (*that, it*). Pronouns are a great invention because they can take the place of nouns to make sentences read more smoothly and to avoid having to repeat the noun they refer to. Imagine having to repeat the same nouns over and over again.

Patty found Patty's purse on the counter where Patty remembered Patty had left Patty's purse.

Pretty ridiculous sounding, right? But without pronouns, what else can we do? Let's recruit some pronouns.

Patty found her purse on the counter where she remembered she had left it.

Much better! Now you know the power of pronouns. Let's look at the different types of pronouns and their roles in a sentence.

PRONOUN PROPERTIES

Pronouns have *cases*, which means they can take different forms depending on their function in a sentence. The three pronoun cases in English are *subjective* (nominative), *objective* (accusative), and *possessive*. *Subjective pronouns* act as subjects, *objective pronouns* act as objects, and *possessive pronouns* show ownership.

Pronouns also come in three "person" forms. First person pronouns refer to the person or group speaking (*I, we*). Second person pronouns refer to the person or group being addressed (*you*). Third person pronouns refer to people or things being spoken about (*she, he, it, they, him, her, them*).

TYPES OF PRONOUNS

FORM	CASES		
	SUBJECTIVE	OBJECTIVE	POSSESSIVE
first person (singular)	I	me	my (mine)
second person (singular / plural)	you	you	your (yours)
third person (singular)	he, she, it	him, her, it	his, her (hers), its
first person (plural)	we	us	our (ours)
third person (plural)	they	them	their (theirs)
interrogative	who	whom	whose

TYPES OF PRONOUNS

Personal pronouns function as subjects and objects in a sentence. *Subject pronouns* serve as the subject in a sentence. They include *I, you, she, he, it, we, you, they*, and *who*. Subject pronouns use the *subjective* case, which means they function like nouns.

Who is going to the cat show?

We like line dancing and stone skipping.

She foraged for snacks in the kitchen.

I am studying for a boat captain's license.

Object pronouns function as objects in a sentence. They include *me, you, him, her, it, us, you, them*, and *whom*. Object pronouns use the *objective* case, which means they act as the direct object or indirect object of a verb or the object of a preposition.

We surmised that the ferret belonged to him. (object of a preposition)

Will you lend me your bowling ball? (indirect object)

I found it! (direct object)

Possessive pronouns show ownership and use the *possessive* case. They include *my, mine, your, yours, her, hers, his, its, ours, your, yours, their*, and *theirs*. Note that possessive pronouns do not use apostrophes. (For more information, see Chapter 18: Possessives.)

Her clever invention wowed the science fair judges.

We chuckled when we perused its contents.

The gigantic snowshoes are mine.

Interrogative pronouns are used in questions. They substitute for a noun as an answer to a question. The five main interrogative pronouns are *who, what, whom, whose,* and *which*. These same pronouns can also end in -ever for more emphasis (*whoever, whatever, whomever, whosever, whichever*).

<u>Who</u> is coming to the game? (<u>Phillip</u> is coming.)

<u>Whose</u> is this? (It's <u>Lucky's</u>.)

<u>Which</u> is better? (<u>Pecan</u> is better.)

<u>What</u> is the quickest route to the chocolate shop? (<u>Cherry Street</u> is the quickest route.)

<u>Whoever</u> is leaving last should turn off the lights.

Demonstrative pronouns reference or point to something in terms of distance or time. They include *this, that, these,* and *those*.

<u>Those</u> are silly shoes.

What is <u>this</u>?

<u>That</u> was what I was telling you!

Reflexive pronouns refer back to the same subject of a sentence and end in -self (singular) or -selves (plural). These pronouns include *myself, himself, herself, itself, yourself, ourselves, yourselves,* and *themselves*.

We helped <u>ourselves</u> to more brownies.

I <u>myself</u> don't mind washing the dog.

They offered to unload the cartons <u>themselves</u>.

Relative pronouns introduce a dependent clause that adds more information about (or relates to) a noun. These pronouns include *who, whom, that, which,* and *whose*. Relative pronouns can introduce essential and nonessential dependent clauses. (See Chapter 19: Independent and Dependent Clauses ("Clawses") for more information.)

The chili, <u>which</u> was too spicy, didn't get eaten.

The folding chairs <u>that</u> we are sitting on are noisy.

The guests <u>whom</u> I invited haven't arrived yet.

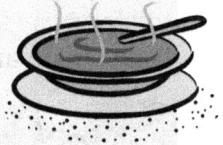

Indefinite pronouns are used to describe indefinite or unspecified people, things, or amounts. They include *all, any, anyone, anybody, anything, both, each, everybody, everyone, everything, few, many, nobody, none, several, someone, somebody,* and *something*. Indefinite pronouns can be singular (*each, anyone*), plural (*both, few, many*), or singular/plural depending on the context (*none, some*). See Chapter 20: Subject–Verb Agreement and Spats for more information.

<u>Anyone</u> can visit the cat topiary park.

<u>Both</u> are reliable pancake recipes.

<u>Few</u> know how to operate the huge forklift.

PRONOUN PICKLES

Even though pronouns are powerful, they can sometimes get writers into a pickle. This happens if pronouns are used incorrectly or are overused. Here are some common pronoun problems to watch for.

1 **Vague pronoun references.** When using pronouns, it's important to be clear about who or what the pronoun is referring to. For example,

The cat licked her paw.

Here it's clear that the pronoun "her" refers to the cat. The word "cat" is called the *antecedent*. Antecedents are words that come before a pronoun that references it. If you don't make it clear who or what a pronoun is referring to, it can confuse and annoy readers as they try to figure out what your sentence means. Errors occur when pronouns are used without an antecedent, the antecedent is too far away from the pronoun to make sense, or the pronoun used is just plain ambiguous. For example,

The students visited the zoo animals, and they were eating bananas.

Here it's unclear what "they" refers to. Who was eating the bananas (the students or the animals)? We can make it clear who was doing what by recasting the sentence and moving the pronoun "who" close to the word it is referencing.

The students visited the zoo animals, who were eating bananas.

Here is another example in which the pronoun reference is vague.

Vague: The classroom had a bulletin board and desks for each student. They were two feet tall.

Clear: The classroom had a bulletin board and student desks that were two feet tall.

In the sentence above, it is now clear that the desks (rather than the students) were two feet tall. Be conscious about the pronouns you use to ensure it's clear which words they refer to.

2 **Wrong pronoun cases.** When using pronouns to fill in for nouns, it's important to use the correct pronoun case (subjective or objective). Pronouns that act as subjects should use the subjective case. Pronouns that act as objects should use the objective case. Errors in case commonly occur in sentences with a mixture of nouns and pronouns.

Incorrect: Please join Carrie and I for the owl hike.
Correct: Please join Carrie and me for the owl hike.
           (*Me* acts as a direct object.)

Incorrect: Grant and me attended the Starfleet conference.
Correct: Grant and I attended the Starfleet conference.
           (*I* acts as a subject.)

TIP: If you're unsure which pronoun case to use, omit the noun temporarily and see if the sentence still makes sense with the pronoun alone.

Incorrect pronoun cases can also crop up with the words *who* and *whom*. *Who* should be used when the word acts as a subject. *Whom* should be used when the word acts as an object of a verb or a preposition. Note that *whom* is not often used in everyday conversation nowadays. In formal writing, however, whom is correct and preferred. Note that *whoever* and *whomever* follow the same rules as *who* and *whom*.

Who ate the last piece of pie?
(*Who* acts as a subject.)

Kathleen, *whom* we all respect, was selected as the chair.
(*Whom* acts as a direct object.)

We will consult with *whoever* is the most knowledgeable.
(*Whoever* acts as an additional subject.)

To *whom* should the report be sent?
(*Whom* acts as the object of a preposition.)

To decide whether to use who/whoever or whom/whomever in a sentence, try replacing the word with "he, she, or they" or "him, her, or them." If he/she/they sounds correct, use *who*. If him/her/them is correct, use whom. In more complex sentences, you may have to rearrange the words so it's clear which word to use.

Who ate the last piece of pie?
(He ate the last piece of pie.)

Kathleen, whom we all respect, was selected as the chair.
(Kathleen, we all respect her, was selected as the chair.)

We will consult with whoever is the most knowledgeable.
(We will consult with (he (who) is the most knowledgeable.)

To whom should the report be sent?
(The report should be sent to them.)

TIP: If the use of whom feels stilted, even though it is grammatically correct, you can sometimes recast the sentence to avoid its use or omit the word altogether.

The auto parts manager whom we contacted is on vacation.

The auto parts manager we contacted is on vacation.

3 **Pronoun wordiness.** The pronouns *it* and *there* can be used in a sentence without referring to a specific noun, for example, "It is snowing" or "There are many reasons for the delay." These expressions have their place in writing, but they can sometimes make a sentence unnecessarily wordy. Notice some of the sentences below use *it* and *there*. These sentences can be strengthened when they are recast to use the main noun instead of extra pronouns.

It is likely to rain tomorrow.

Rain is likely tomorrow.

There are three radio stations in the city.

The city has three radio stations.

There exist three varieties of the sunflower.

The sunflower has three varieties.

There was an odd odor in the garage.

An odd odor lingered in the garage.

PRONOUN PRECISION

Pronouns can be perfect substitutes for nouns, making writing less wordy and more agile. Because they essentially act as nouns, pronouns can function like nouns as subjects and objects. They can also indicate ownership when used in the possessive sense. To master pronouns is to master their cases and fully understand how they are used in a sentence. Using clear pronoun references and avoiding wordy pronoun expressions can make your writing crisper and sharper. Now that's being precise about pronouns.

7

ADJECTIVES
FRILLS AND FRIPPERIES

Adjectives more fully describe nouns and pronouns. They can richly depict people, places, and things: *craggy, smoky, windswept, tattered, ghostly, silken, resplendent, sudsy, effervescent,* and *pungent.* Like a costume and makeup crew, adjectives dress up nouns and pronouns with various frills and decorations, to make them more memorable and specific. Sensory adjectives in particular paint a vivid picture for readers and set the right mood for a story or essay.

TYPES OF ADJECTIVES

Adjectives come in several varieties. They describe, specify, limit, quantify, and qualify a noun or pronoun. Adjectives indicate the size, shape, color, sound, and amount of whatever they're describing.

The _____ cowboy is the star of the show.
(adjective)

Attributive adjectives appear before the noun they are describing. They describe the color, shape, sound, size, and other attributes of nouns.

dilapidated house

gigantic pumpkin

fierce Chihuahua

whimsical camel

Predicate adjectives are descriptive adjectives that come *after* nouns and pronouns. These sentences use "to be" verbs (*is, are, was,* etc.).

Cats are fluffy.

She is exhausted.

That odor is noxious.

The map was indecipherable.

Compound adjectives (also called compound modifiers) contain two or more words and are often hyphenated.

mind-boggling puzzle

half-hearted laugh

ticky-tacky lawsuit

ADJECTIVES: FRILLS AND FRIPPERIES

Coordinate adjectives are multiple adjectives used to describe a noun. If the adjectives are of equal rank, commas or an *and* can be used between them.

> a <u>brisk</u>, <u>spirited</u> pickleball tournament
>
> the <u>long</u> and <u>winding</u> lavender walkway
>
> the <u>reluctant</u>, <u>absent-minded</u> accountant

Commas are omitted if the adjectives are not of equal rank (e.g., if an adjective describes a unit formed by a second adjective and noun).

> <u>sunny</u> garden apartment
>
> <u>boring</u> business meeting
>
> <u>glamorous</u> speaking engagement

Proper adjectives describe the place or origin of something using an adjective form of a proper noun.

> <u>German</u> history
>
> <u>Ethiopian</u> coffee
>
> <u>Shakespearian</u> sonnet

Absolute, *comparative*, and *superlative* adjectives show comparisons.

> tall, taller, tallest
>
> good, better, best
>
> sleek, sleeker, sleekest

Adjectives can show a quantity or number of things, either specifically and numerically (for example, 157, thirty-four, six) or indefinitely (*all, any, both, either, few, half, many, much, neither, several, some*).

forty-seven curious geese

many unanswered questions

some cinnamon bagels

Participial adjectives contain verbs that can function as adjectives to modify a noun or a pronoun. They often end in -ing or -ed.

the undulating flag

the complicated chipmunk

burnt marshmallows

the steaming casserole

ADJECTIVES IN ACTION

Adjectives are a fascinating part of speech, but it's important to know how and when to use them to help your writing. In many cases, adjectives are extra "fluff" words. They are not absolutely essential for a sentence to be complete. However, when adjectives are chosen thoughtfully, they can add outstanding flavor, texture, and color to nouns and pronouns. And without adjectives, life is like a home without cat toys: lacking a bit of fun and excitement. Here are a few pointers for using adjectives.

1 **Pick the most descriptive, sensory adjectives you can find.** Be selective with adjectives. Choose ones that are the most specific and apt for the person, place, or thing you're describing. Tap into the five senses to describe how something looks, sounds, feels, tastes, and smells. Some of the best adjectives are onomatopoeic (they make a sound): *hissing, clanging, buzzing, chittering.* Pick adjectives that are packed with meaning and energy—the ones that make your hair stand up and your nose twitch. Pair vivid adjectives with strong nouns and verbs. For more advice on using sensory nouns and verbs, see Chapters 3 and 5.

Carole ate the <u>gingery</u>, <u>garlicky</u> soup with gusto.

The blast of <u>frigid</u> air stunned him into silence.

The <u>wide-eyed</u> cat investigated the <u>churring</u> sound.

We basked in the <u>sparkling</u>, <u>turquoise</u> waters of Greece.

I finished the <u>jaw-dropping</u> book in one evening.

2. **Don't overdo adjectives.** Using extra adjectives can add too many unnecessary accessories and fripperies to one noun or pronoun. With excessive adjectives, writing starts to look gaudy and feel heavy. Also, a string of adjectives with similar meanings sounds redundant. In some cases, it is best to replace multiple adjectives with a stronger noun.

Overdone: The small, diminutive, quaint house was charming.
Better: The cottage was charming.

Overdone: The mountainous rocks in the canyon were gigantic and towering.
Better: The canyon walls towered above us.

Also, in general avoid adding "very" or "really" to adjectives. Adjectives are usually stronger without it. If you need to use *very* or *really* with an adjective, it suggests the adjective, noun, or verb you're using isn't strong enough to stand on its own.

3. **Don't use an adjective to modify a verb.** Adjectives modify nouns and pronouns. Adverbs, on the other hand, modify verbs. If you mix up their functions, it can create a grammar error. This happens if you use an adverb when you should use an adjective, and vice versa. Let's see some examples.

Incorrect: He tried to speak <u>louder</u>.
(*Louder* is an adjective. If we want to describe *how* he spoke (a verb), we need an adverb instead of an adjective.)

Correct: He tried to speak <u>more loudly</u>.
(*More loudly* functions as an adverb modifying the verb *speak*. It tells *how* he spoke.)

Correct: He was <u>loud</u> when he spoke.
(<u>Loud</u> in this case is a predicate adjective, an adjective that comes after a "to be" verb and a noun or pronoun. See p 66.)

Incorrect: They play football <u>real</u> well.
(*Real* is an adjective. If we want to describe *how* they play, we need an adverb instead of an adjective.)

Correct: They play football really well.
(*Really well* functions as an adverb modifying the verb *play*. It indicates *how* they play.)

Correct: They play football quite well.
(*Quite well* functions as an adverb modifying the verb *play*. It indicates *how* they play.)

To check if an adjective or adverb is used correctly, find the word it is supposed to be modifying. If the word is a noun or pronoun, then use an adjective to describe it. If it's a verb or another adverb, use an adverb to describe it.

In the next chapter, we'll discuss adverbs in more detail and see how they can give verbs more power and punch.

Head Scratcher

If *adverbs* modify verbs and *adjectives* modify nouns, why aren't adjectives called *adnouns*?

According to *Merriam-Webster's*, the word *adjective* was first used in the 14th century. The word is actually a shortened form of the phrase *noun adjective*, which comes from the Latin *nomen adjectivum*. *Nomen* means "name," *ad* means "to or toward," and *jacere* means "throw." Thus, the modern, shortened term *adjective* means to throw something, in this case, toward a name—like a noun's modifier.

Incidentally, the word *adverb* also comes from the Latin *ad* meaning "to" and *verbum* meaning "word"—which surprisingly isn't a very descriptive definition for *adverb*. So it seems the word *adjective* has a livelier meaning than the word *adverb*. However, they are both useful for describing or modifying other words.

8

ADVERBS
GO AFFABLY

Maggie rides her bike _____ .
(adverb)

I f adjectives are like a costume crew for nouns, *adverbs* are like special effects specialists for *verbs*. Adverbs describe *how, when, where,* and *to what extent.* They more fully describe *verbs* rather than *nouns.* This is why they are called "adverbs" because their primary function is to "add" to verbs (from Latin *ad* meaning *to* + *verbum* meaning "word"). However, adverbs can also modify other adverbs, adjectives, phrases, or whole sentences. Adverbs can be single words (*calmly, breathlessly, never*), phrases (*every day, as soon as possible*), and clauses (*when the archeologists arrive*).

Most adverbs are formed by adding –ly to an existing word (*rapid > rapidly, unflinching > unflinchingly*). If an adjective ends in –y, then –ily is usually added to create the adverb (*easy > easily, dreamy >*

dreamily). However, some common adverbs do not end in –ly. These include *again, also, soon, never, often, too, very, rather*, and *well*.

TYPES OF ADVERBS

Adverbs that modify verbs. These are the most common types of adverbs. Look for the verbs in a sentence, and notice that adverbs give the verbs an extra bit of zing and specificity.

> We navigated <u>briskly</u> through the rapids.
>
> She pounded the drums <u>triumphantly</u>.
>
> He spoke <u>haltingly</u> about the mysterious guests.

Adverbs that modify adjectives. These types of adverbs extend the meaning of an adjective by indicating *how much* or *to what extent*.

> <u>stunningly</u> beautiful
>
> <u>extraordinarily</u> wrinkled
>
> <u>shockingly</u> stinky

Adverbs that modify other adverbs. These types of adverbs pair with another adverb to modify a verb. They indicate *how, to what extent, how long, how often, when,* and *where*.

> <u>extremely</u> slowly
>
> <u>nearly</u> always
>
> <u>rather</u> pitifully

Adverbs that modify clauses or sentences. Clause or sentence adverbs modify the whole clause or sentence they appear in. These adverbs include commentary words such as *obviously, fortunately, luckily, frankly, unfortunately*, and *presumably*. These adverbs can be moved around in the sentence without changing the meaning.

Frankly, we've tasted better omelets.

Presumably, I can return the garden hoe if I don't like it.

Obviously, I need more practice hitting the high notes.

Interrogative adverbs are used in questions. These adverbs include the words *when, where, why*, and *how*. They answer questions about *time, place, degree, quantity, reason*, or *manner*.

When are we going to get the new dog for Kathleen's birthday?

Where is the backgammon game?

Why are my shoes missing again?

How did you solve that math problem?

Relative adverbs are used to start a dependent clause. (A dependent clause is an incomplete thought or sentence fragment.) Relative adverbs include *when, where, why*, and *how*. They are part of a clause that indicates a time, place, or reason.

Many cats like to be petted when they are sleepy.

This is the building where Kerry went to school.

He jumped when the bell rang.

We don't know how the window got broken.

ADVERB ADVICE

1. **Choose descriptive adverbs but avoid overdoing them.** Use adverbs selectively and sparingly so they stand out and provide the best special effects for your sentences. Think about *how, where, when,* or *to what degree* an action takes place to more thoroughly describe a scene. Use all of your senses (see, hear, touch, smell, and taste) to select the best adverbs. Avoid overburdening a sentence with too many adverbs. If you use a strong verb, you may not need any adverbs.

Overdone: We walked slowly and leisurely down the hall.
Better: We strolled down the hall.

Overdone: He looked curiously and closely at the machine.
Better: He peered at the machine.

2. **Know when to use an adverb and when to use an adjective.** Adverbs are used to modify verbs, adjectives, and other adverbs. Adjectives are used to modify nouns and pronouns. Mixing them up could create an unintended meaning. An exception to this rule is for linking verbs, such as *seems, tastes, feels, smells, sounds,* and *appears.* Linking verbs most often require adjectives rather than adverbs after them.

Incorrect: The <u>eagerly</u> crowd packed the stands. (*Eagerly* is an adverb, so it shouldn't be used to modify *crowd*, a noun.)

Correct: The <u>eager</u> crowd packed the stands. (*Eager* correctly modifies *crowd*, a noun.)

Incorrect: This fish tastes badly. (*Tastes* is used as a linking verb here, so it requires an adjective rather than an adverb after it. If you use the adverb *badly*, you're saying that the fish's sense of taste isn't good.)

Correct: This fish tastes bad. (*Tastes* acts as a linking verb connecting the noun *fish* to the adjective *bad*.)

ADVERBS INDICATE HOW, WHEN, WHERE, AND TO WHAT EXTENT

HOW (IN WHAT MANNER)

quietly, nervously, quickly, reluctantly, frantically, fast, well, mysteriously, blindly, frightfully, curiously, thoroughly, deeply, briskly, carefully, abruptly

WHEN

now, soon, often, today, tomorrow, rarely, promptly, immediately, regularly, repeatedly, sometimes, continuously, right away, never, daily, yesterday

WHERE

everywhere, above, beyond, below, upstairs, outside, nearby, anywhere, under, up, down, behind, away, near, there

TO WHAT EXTENT

nearly, totally, completely, barely, almost, exceedingly, absolutely, far, practically, quite, very, somewhat, too, utterly, virtually, simply

9

PREPOSITIONS IN HIGH POSITIONS

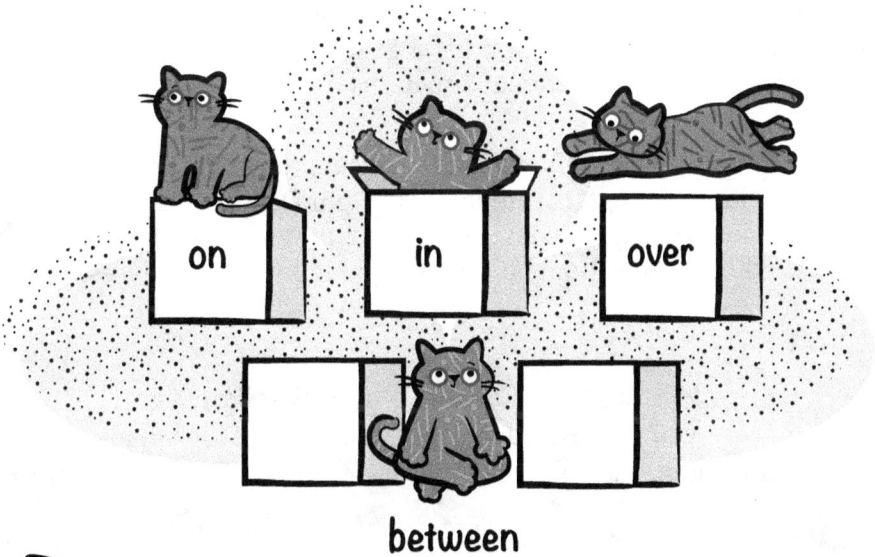

ehold the lowly preposition: a small, seemingly insignificant word. In fact, prepositions are very popular words in sentences. For instance, the prepositions *of* and *to* are the third and fourth most commonly used words in the English language (behind *the* and *be*). The most popular prepositions include *of, at, by, for, from, in, on, with, to, across, around, below, between, during, over, toward, under,* and *within*. Prepositions are convenient for showing position, time, direction, and location. They are most often used in prepositional phrases that include a noun or a pronoun (the object of the preposition). For example,

during the chess match

across the floor

at the abode

a bundle of flowers

Prepositions are highly specific words: *on the chair* means something different than *behind the chair* or *under the chair*. In general, native English speakers intuitively know which preposition is best to use for a given situation. However, students learning English sometimes struggle with the correct preposition to use. Also, preposition meanings and usage can vary regionally. It's helpful to read widely so you get a good feel for how prepositions are used correctly in different situations.

A common problem in writing is using unnecessary or extra prepositions. Strings of prepositional phrases can make writing wordy and convoluted and obscure a sentence's meaning. Notice the needless prepositional phrases in the following sentences.

Wordy: In order to avoid a sum of money collected as a penalty, you are advised to submit payment of the bill in full without delay.

Better: To avoid a fee, pay your bill immediately.

Wordy: We are of the opinion that the lack of suitable feline snacks in this household contributes to a range of issues of concern.

Better: We are out of good cat snacks.

Another common error is using extra, unnecessary propositions (especially *at* and *to*) in sentences. For instance,

Incorrect: Where is he **at**?

Correct: Where is he?

Incorrect: We instructed the cat to get off **of** the table.

Correct: We instructed the cat to get off the table.

LIST OF COMMON PREPOSITIONS

RELATIONSHIP	EXAMPLES
location	*about, above, across, after, against, ahead of, along, amid, among, at, below, beneath, beside, between, beyond, by, close to, down, in, inside, near, next to, off, on, out, outside, over, through, under, up, upon, with, within*
time	*after, around, at, before, during, in, on, past, prior to, since, throughout, till, until*
movement	*across, along, around, away from, back, down, forward, into, onto, past, through, to, toward, up, up to*
other	*about, according to, as, as well as, because of, by means of, by way of, concerning, despite, except, for, from, in addition to, in place of, of, per, regarding, via, with*

Head Scratcher ENDING WITH A PREPOSITION

Why are we so afraid to end a sentence with a preposition?

"A preposition is something never to end a sentence with," advised William Safire, the American grammarian and *The New York Times* columnist. This rule is so well received by most teachers and students of American grammar that very few writers question it. The truth is this rule is not ironclad. In many cases, it is perfectly acceptable to end a sentence with a preposition. It's just that putting a preposition by itself at the end of a sentence sometimes sounds awkward, and many people think there must be a rule against it. Not so. In fact, rewriting a sentence to avoid a preposition at the end can make a sentence sound even worse. So, it's best to go with what sounds good to the ear, rather than creating a hard and fast rule against prepositions at the end of a sentence. This reminds us of another interesting quote from Mr. Safire: "Never assume the obvious is true." Well, of course, the Earth *looks* flat.

10

JUNCTIONS OF CONJUNCTIONS

Kit_____Kat love(s) chocolate_____vanilla ice cream.
   (conjunction)   (conjunction)

Conjunctions join words and groups of words together. The word *conjunction* is related to the words *conjoin*, meaning to join or combine, and *junction*, meaning a place where things are joined. Conjunctions are used in lists of items and to link different clauses or phrases together. Conjunctions are also useful to indicate the relationships between different parts of a sentence and to provide smooth transitions between clauses.

TYPES OF CONJUNCTIONS

Coordinating conjunctions join words, phrases, and clauses of equal ranking. These conjunctions include *and, or,* and *but,* among others. In a list of three or more items, a comma is generally used before the coordinating conjunction. This is called a series comma (or serial or Oxford comma). (See Chapter 14: Comma Corral (and Parentheses too) for more information about series commas.)

They will go kayaking, fly a kite, <u>or</u> build a sand castle.

We ordered a chisel, a mallet, <u>and</u> a sander.

Madeline found a wooly worm, a feather, <u>and</u> a ribbon on her walk.

Importantly, coordinating conjunctions are used to connect two independent clauses (complete thoughts) together. A good way to remember all of the coordinating conjunctions is with the acronym FANBOYS that stands for For, And, Nor, But, Or, Yet, and So. When you use these words to join two independent clauses, you should use a comma before them:

For: Teresa reads many suspenseful novels, for they enrich her life with adventure.

And: The river is lined with black willows, and it attracts many birds.

Nor: I refuse to wear mittens, nor do I like scarves.

But: I raced to the door, but the dog ran out.

Or: He could have hot cocoa, or he could shovel the snow.

Yet: I don't mind walking in the rain, yet I regret getting my new shoes muddy.

So: Shana was feeling sleepy, so she went home after the play.

JUNCTIONS OF CONJUNCTIONS

Subordinating conjunctions link a dependent clause to an independent clause. Examples of subordinating conjunctions include *although, after, because, even though, unless, until, while,* and *if*. These conjunctions show different relationships between clauses and provide a smooth and interesting transition of ideas. Subordinating conjunctions (underlined below) appear at the beginning of a dependent clause (an incomplete thought), which can come before or after an independent clause (a complete thought).

Although I broke my glasses, I still enjoyed the hula hoop concert.

We waited until his laughing fit subsided.

Mary Ann sang, while Susie played the accordion.

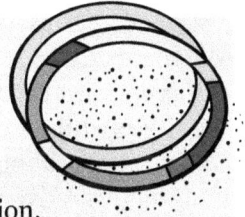

Paired conjunctions. Paired (or correlative) conjunctions are used in pairs. These include *either...or, neither...nor, if...then, not only... but also,* and *both...and.* Paired conjunctions are useful for conveying momentum and rhythm in a sentence. If the second paired conjunction separates two independent clauses, then a comma is used before it.

Both apricots and peaches are delicious.

Not only can my cat high five, but also she retrieves toys.

Neither a pipe wrench nor a crescent wrench will fix this problem.

Conjunctive adverbs. Conjunctive adverbs are adverbs, not true conjunctions. However, they can act like conjunctions when they link independent clauses together. Examples include *therefore, however, namely, eventually, furthermore, consequently, in fact,* and *for example.* Conjunctive adverbs (underlined below) are very useful and descriptive words because they signal time, order, contrast, consequence of events, and additions between clauses.

We thought about opening a cat skateboarding park; <u>eventually</u>, we came to our senses.

The letter is full of errors; <u>furthermore</u>, it is dull.

My cat loves to climb; <u>in fact</u>, he thinks the cabinets are his tree house.

When using conjunctions, it's important to use the proper punctuation around them so your meaning is clear. See Chapter 19: Independent and Dependent Clauses ("Clawses") for more information about clauses, subordinating conjunctions, and conjunctive adverbs. See a summary of the different types of conjunctions on the following page.

CONJUNCTION ASSUMPTION

If you have the gumption,
You can choose the proper conjunction
To link phrases and words
From the sublime to the absurd.

And henceforth and hitherto
Add a conjunctive adverb or two
To give your sentences some style
And smooth the lines meanwhile.

As you can see, conjunctions are incredibly handy words for joining words and phrases and providing smooth, even elegant, transitions between clauses. With conjunctions and conjunctive adverbs, readers can quickly grasp the connections between thoughts that a writer is trying to convey. Conjunctions can also help you understand how to punctuate your sentences correctly—depending on the types of words and clauses they join. Thus, we can make the presumption, you'll always find the perfect conjunction.

TYPES OF CONJUNCTIONS

TYPE	FUNCTION	EXAMPLES
coordinating conjunctions	join words, phrases, and clauses of equal ranking	*for, and, nor, but, or, yet, so* (FANBOYS)
subordinating conjunctions	link a dependent clause to an independent clause	*after, although, as, because, before, even though, if, once, since, that, though, unless, until, whereas, while, which* (see p 154)
paired conjunctions	used in pairs	*either...or, neither... nor, not only...but also, both...and, if...then*
conjunctive adverbs	join independent clauses together to show relationships, such as time, order, contrast, consequence of events, and additions	*accordingly, as a result, conversely, eventually, finally, for example, furthermore, hence, however, in addition, in fact, instead, meanwhile, moreover, namely, otherwise, thus, therefore* (see p 150)

11

INTERJECTIONS, YAHOO!

Hooray! This is the last main part of speech, the interjection. Interjections are bursts of expression that convey surprise, alarm, delight, outrage, or other emotion or opinion. They are single words or phrases that add a bit of commentary to writing. They often end in exclamation points or question marks, or they are set off by commas. As asides or outbursts, interjections are useful, especially in dialogue, because they reflect how people really talk. Interjections can be humorous or unexpected and give writing a bit of pop and style. Amirite?

Yikes, what a strange day!

Wow!

What?!

Oops, um, I forgot your name.

Parts of Speech Cast & Crew

NOUNS

Name Producers and Stars

apple
Mt Rushmore
candle
Florida
Elizabeth

Job: Provide names for people, places, things

VERBS

Directors of Action & Linking

Job: Provide action; link and help other verbs

PRONOUNS

Stunt Doubles

she
they
me

Job: Serve as stand-ins for nouns

ADJECTIVES

Costume Designers

Job: Provide costumes, hair, and makeup for nouns

Supporting Roles

Adverbs: **Special Effects Specialists**
Job: Add sound, light, and special effects for verbs

Prepositions: **Logistics and Location Managers**
Job: Indicate positions and relationships of other words

Conjunctions: **Relationship Coordinators**
Job: Link together words, phrases, and clauses

Interjections: **Animated Commentators**
Job: Provide exclamations, sudden outbursts, and side comments

SUM OF ITS PARTS

As you can see from reviewing this section, parts of speech are amazing tools for writing. They work together as building blocks for constructing sentences and communicating effectively. Take the time to get to know each part of speech well. The more you understand each part, the more you'll know how to create delightful sentences and punctuate them correctly. Like cats, each part of speech has its own personality. Like cats, each part is unique, intriguing, and lovable.

We now shift our attention to punctuation, those useful, intriguing, but sometimes confusing, marks in sentences.

SECTION 2

PUSSYCAT PUNCTUATION

PERIODS AND OTHER POWERFUL MARKS

SEMICOLONS AND COLONS: ROLLING STOPS AND SHOWSTOPPERS

COMMA CORRAL (AND PARENTHESES TOO)

ALL ABOUT APOSTROPHES

MAD DASHES AND HYPHEN HYPE

QUOTE-UNQUOTE

12

PERIODS AND OTHER POWERFUL MARKS

If you want to learn punctuation well, it helps to observe a cat. Cats use punctuation marks all the time to communicate. With their claws, they scratch out commas and apostrophes to mark things important to them (for instance, "Kiki's treats, toys, and brushes"). Cats can also demonstrate their grasp of dashes, full stops, and even semicolon-like rolling stops—across a shiny floor. And their expressive tails always make a statement or pose a question.

If you look closely, punctuation marks are a kind of musical notation in text. They indicate timings, breaks, and word dynamics in sentences in the form of pauses, stops, interruptions, asides, and other flourishes (for more about this, see p 101). Also note that punctuation marks didn't just fall out of the sky from somewhere. They were invented and refined over centuries to bring order and elegance to the written English language. They help signal a writer's intended meaning and tone, for instance, by the precise placement of commas and periods. They also give writing a bit of flair and panache—through the use of colons, dashes, ellipses, and so on.

Good punctuation can help you write better because it makes what you've written more understandable, and it helps prevent confusion. For example, the sentence "Cats search for the missing pizza slice." means something quite different than "Cats: search for the missing pizza slice." Hmm.

For punctuation advice, Punctsie, aka the Punctuation Pussycat, is a good teacher. Punctsie is very punctual about learning punctuation. She never misses a lesson, and that's what makes her a wiz at punctuation. Her advice will pop up throughout this section, to help you mark all of your sentences with style.

MORE ABOUT PUNCTSIE

A cat named Punctsie had a dot on her side,
And three little kittens she licked when they cried.
She had five claws
On her two front paws.
But counting her whiskers, no one has tried!

In this chapter, let's look at punctuation marks that have the biggest punch: periods, question marks, and exclamation points. We'll also examine the handy three-dot ellipsis.

PERIODLY

One of the most important punctuation marks in writing is the period. A period is used at the end of a sentence. For instance,

Carlisle was a careless mouse.

This is a complete sentence.
A sentence is a complete thought. However, suppose you wrote

Carlisle's friend Freddy, who is very fast.

This is only a phrase, not a complete sentence, because it doesn't tell us what Fast Freddy did. A period at the end of that phase is confusing because it's only a sentence fragment, and it leaves the reader suspended in mid-air. Let's complete the thought:

Carlisle's friend Freddy, who is very fast, races to the mouse door.

Now we have a complete sentence, with a period at the end, and the reader has the full information. A period is sometimes called a Full Stop, which means the reader can pause after the sentence and let the complete thought sink in. Punctsie uses one middle claw to make a period after her sentences (and she can be *rather dramatic* about it, too).

If you write a sentence and leave out the period at the end, or run sentences together, it can confuse readers or make you look careless. When you write, it's seldom good to look careless. *If you're a mouse, it's never good to look careless around a cat.* However, even Punctsie herself sometimes forgets to use periods at the end of her sentences—if she's in a hurry zipping through the house like a crazy cat. She even runs her words together at times (for example, "didyouseethatbunny?!"). But we digress....

Note that periods can be used at the end of phrases or sentence fragments, for effect. However, phrases and fragments are used only informally in writing. Just for fun. To add a bit of style. For formal writing, however, it's best to write in complete sentences and punctuate them with a period. Full stop.

Beyond their use in sentences, periods appear after abbreviations, such as "in." for inch, "a.m." for ante meridiem, or "Prof." for Professor. They are generally not used in acronyms, which are words formed by combining initial letters of multiple words, such as "NASA" for National Aeronautics and Space Administration and "radar" for RAdio Detection And Ranging.

QUESTION MARKS ARE THE ANSWER

A question mark is a cat's favorite punctuation because she spends most of her waking hours being curious. She roams around the house or yard all day asking Who, What, When, Where, How, and Why. Her body language gives her away; her tail is in the shape of a question mark. This is a good thing. When someone is questioning what they see, hear, smell, feel, or taste, like an inquisitive cat, they get more answers. Some answers they get are not always correct. However, the more they think about things to investigate, the better they do in their research. Also, one question can lead to other more interesting questions.

Questions can be a fun tool in your writing. Why is this? Well, questions provide a bit of variety and suspense. Readers want to know the answers to the questions you pose. Questions also give writing a different lilt and rising inflection, which adds to the musicality of written and spoken text. Wouldn't you agree?

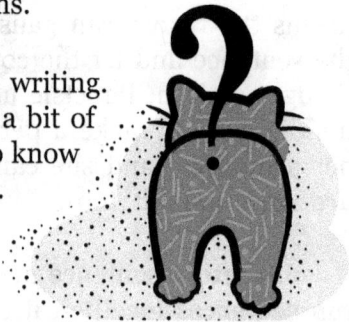

When you use question marks, remember to use them only after actual questions. Not all sentences that begin with who, what, when, where, or why are questions requiring a question mark. Sometimes, these sentences are actually statements. For example,

Statement: Why I keep losing my keys is beyond me.
Question: Why do I keep losing my keys?

Statement: I wonder where all the pie went.
Question: "Where did all the pie go?" she wondered aloud.

Note: some questions (perhaps the ones above) are *rhetorical* questions in which the asker does not expect a direct response. Rhetorical questions are useful to emphasize a point or encourage reflection. And sometimes they are just self-evident and humorous. Isn't that interesting? (Yes, that's being rhetorical.)

TO THEE I EXCLAIM

Do you remember how a cat's tail often reminds you of a question mark? Well, a cat's tail looks very different when she gets excited. Then, it shoots straight up like an exclamation point. It's as if she's shouting "Wow!" like she really has something to exclaim. When Punctsie is bored or sleeping, her tail is down. However, when she sees a mouse or a chipmunk run by, her tail goes straight up, like an exclamation point.

In writing, you can use exclamation points for a powerful impact. They can appear after a complete sentence, a phrase, or a single word to signal to readers your amazement, surprise, or other strong emotion. Exclamation points also can be used in interjections, which are words or phrases that express a spontaneous reaction (see Chapter 11: Interjections, Yahoo! for more details on interjections). For example,

What a mess!	Wow!	Hooray!
Chloe, get off the table!	Double drat!	

Exclamation points are a fun punctuation mark that can jazz up your writing. However, use them sparingly and only when you really mean it. Otherwise, too many exclamation points can become tiresome to readers and will begin to lose their punch, like a stale joke that fails to land.

DOT DOT DOT: ELLIPSIS

An ellipsis (plural: ellipses) is the three little dots (...) that indicate that words have been omitted in a sentence or paragraph. They are often used to shorten direct quotations to emphasize the important content. An ellipsis can also be used to indicate a slight pause, an unfinished idea, or a thought that trails off into silence, leaving the reader to fill in the details.

Ralph Waldo Emerson wrote, "...adopt the pace of Nature. Her secret is patience."

"Courage...What makes the elephant charge his tusk in the misty mist, or the dusky dusk? Courage." –Cowardly Lion, from *The Wizard of Oz*

I was out of options on the snowy highway. Or so I thought....

TIP: If the three dots of an ellipsis come at the end of a sentence, add a final period (for a total of four) to the end of that sentence.

Astronaut Mae Jemison said, "Don't let anyone rob you of your imagination, your creativity, or your curiosity.... It's your life. Go on and do all you can with it, and make it the life you want to live."

THE MUSICAL-LIKE PAUSES OF PUNCTUATION

PUNCTUATION	LENGTH OF PAUSE	USES
comma, parentheses	**1** beat (slight pause)	Separates words, phrases, clauses; adds clarity
semicolon	**2** beats (rolling stop)	Links two related sentences together
M dash, colon	**3** beats (semistop)	Expands a thought, explains more fully, sets up drama, provides style
period, question mark, exclamation point	**4** beats (full stop)	Used after a complete sentence, phrase, or word
ellipsis	varies	Denotes omitted text, a pause, or an unfinished thought

MUSICAL MARKS

Punctuation marks are musical-like rests in text that tell readers when to pause and for how long. As such, they add crispness and flair to writing. In this chapter, we reviewed periods, exclamation points, and question marks that act as full (four-beat) stops. They completely pause a sentence to allow a thought to sink in. An ellipsis also creates a pause, but it can vary in time from a few beats signaling missing words to a long, undetermined suspension of time....

In the coming chapters, we'll review the semicolon, which adds a short, two-beat pause (akin to a rolling stop) to link several thoughts together. And we'll discuss the colon, which adds a longer, three-beat pause (a semistop) to provide drama. Finally, we'll cover the basics of commas and parentheses, which add slight pauses and asides, giving writing a satisfying rhythm.

13

SEMICOLONS AND COLONS
ROLLING STOPS AND SHOWSTOPPERS

Somewhere between the short pause of a comma and the full stop of a period lies the rolling stop of a semicolon. A comma lightly pauses your sentence like you would slightly slow down your car to make a turn. The period brings your sentence to a full stop, like at a red light. A semicolon pauses your sentence like you would brake if an animal ran in front of your car—not a complete stop but a definite slowdown nonetheless, akin to a rolling stop.

ROLLING-STOP SEMICOLONS

SEMICOLON

● ← Stop

, ← Pause

If you look closely at a semicolon (;), it is a rather peculiar punctuation mark that is a half period and half comma. The period part of a semicolon indicates it can act like a period to complete a thought. The comma part of the semicolon is like a cat's claw that hooks one sentence to another sentence. *Thus, semicolons are useful for linking two related sentences together.* The sentence following a semicolon cannot get away because it is being snagged by the first sentence. For example,

Punctsie doesn't like to get her paws wet; instead, she likes to sit by the pond to watch the tadpoles.

Notice the sentences before and after the semicolon are related ones that could stand on their own using a period after each. However, the semicolon joins them to show the reader they belong together. When two sentences are joined together by a semicolon, the semicolon acts as a kind of period for the first sentence. The second sentence that follows a semicolon begins with a lowercase word to show it is actually part of one big sentence formed by two complete sentences (or independent clauses) joined by a semicolon. We will discuss independent clauses in Chapter 19.

Semicolons can be a bit tricky, and they may seem intimidating and fussy. Punctsie can often tell if someone went to college if she sees semicolons in their writing. However, you don't have to have a college degree to use semicolons. They are precise and useful, especially to show relationships between two sentences. If used correctly, semicolons can add a bit of sophistication to your writing. And what cool cat doesn't want to look sophisticated?

SEMICOLONS AND COLONS: ROLLING STOPS AND SHOWSTOPPERS

Here are a few rules for using semicolons.

1. **Use semicolons to link two related sentences (independent clauses) together without using a conjunction (such as *and* or *or*).**

It was a very rainy day; our trip to the amusement park was postponed.

She collects rare seashells; her favorites are the orange Lion's Paw scallop shell and the pretty little Scotch Bonnet.

The play about the shipwreck had many singing parts; nearly every kid got to participate.

2. **Use semicolons between two related sentences (independent clauses) linked by expressions that show relationships such as *however, for example, accordingly, thus, nevertheless, so, moreover, consequently,* and *instead.***

You can still enter the silly limerick contest; however, the deadline is tomorrow.

We gather many accessories when we go sledding; for example, mittens, boots, and earmuffs are handy.

That flower is very fragrant; moreover, it attracts hummingbirds.

TIP: Use a semicolon rather than a comma between two complete sentences (independent clauses). Otherwise, you'll create a run-on sentence (aka, a grammatical train wreck). For example,

Incorrect: Their robot performed well, however, the competition was fierce. (a run-on sentence)

Correct: Their robot performed well; however, the competition was fierce.

3 **Use semicolons in lists with internal commas.**

Short-haired cat breeds include Russian Blue, American short-hair, and Ocicat; medium-haired breeds include Chartreux, Ragamuffin, and Siberian; and long-haired breeds include Maine Coon, Persian, and Turkish Van.

4 **Do not use a semicolon when you mean to use a colon.** A semicolon partially stops the sentence instead of further explaining or announcing something, as a colon would do.

Incorrect: He spotted several bright stars in the night sky; Betelgeuse, Vega, and Capella.

Correct: He spotted several bright stars in the night sky: Betelgeuse, Vega, and Capella.

5 **Do not use a semicolon between independent and dependent clauses.** A comma, rather than a semicolon, is needed between an independent clause and a dependent clause. Otherwise, it will create a sentence fragment.

Incorrect: Coneflowers love the sun; whereas, columbines grow happily in shade.

Correct: Coneflowers love the sun, whereas columbines grow happily in shade.

Incorrect: I raked up most of the leaves in the yard; although, tomorrow there will be many more.

Correct: I raked up most of the leaves in the yard, although tomorrow there will be many more.

COLONS: EXPLAINERS AND SHOWSTOPPERS

Cats don't believe in equality. One cat is always better than another: faster, more clever, sleepier, hungrier, sweeter, cuddlier, or just better-looking. Also, a cat is way better than any other animal, according to a cat. If you have a cat, you know this is what she believes. Don't bother to ask her about it.

However, one thing all punctuation pussycats agree on is this: a colon (:) can act like an equal sign (=). When you use a colon in a sentence, you are often showing your reader that what you wrote before the colon is equivalent to what you wrote after the colon. For example,

Punctsie is prettier than the cats who live across the street: Annabell, Felina, and FooFoo.

Punctsie is quite superior to the animal next door: a noisy dog named Ralph.

Colons are also handy when you want to show a list of similar items or explain something in more detail. For example,

Dogs like to spend their whole day doing what they think is fun: chasing Frisbees, gnawing on old bones, or barking at perfect strangers.

Cats like to spend their day doing what isn't necessary: sampling gourmet cat food, sleeping on the hood of a warm car, or waiting for a chipmunk to make a mistake.

Notice how colons help further explain things by expanding on a thought and giving additional examples. By using colons, you are adding more facts to help make your case. For example, colons help a lawyer cleverly lay out evidence in court. He might say (to expand on T. S. Eliot's famous poem *Macavity: The Mystery Cat*), "Macavity the Cat is surely a thief: when we looked in the jewel box, all the pearls were gone; when we looked for our car, it was gone; when we opened the refrigerator, all the cream was gone!" However, the judge might say, "That is NOT very good evidence: when these things go missing, *Macavity's not there!*" As you can see, colons give a sentence a not-quite-full-stop pause to signal something dramatic may follow it. This "showstopper" quality gives readers pause: they wait to see what follows the colon.

In general, colons are used only after complete sentences, although some style guides allow their use for incomplete sentences. Colons are also used after words or phrases (such as in titles) and in dialogue, verses, times, and citations. For example,

Space: the final frontier

2 Timothy 1:7

9:45

Captain Picard: "Things are only impossible until they are not."

The world record for the backward running marathon is 3:38:27.

The ratio of cats to dogs in my house is 4:1.

As we wrap up semicolons and colons in this chapter, remember that each type of mark has its place. It's important to respect what each can do and use it correctly. Then, you can avail yourself of the precision and clarity that semicolons and colons can bring to your writing.

Now let's turn our attention to commas and parentheses—the shortest but two of the most common types of pauses in sentences.

Head Scratcher **PUNCTUATION IN THE DIGITAL AGE**

In the digital age, people are in a hurry. Thoughts are often run together in messages in a free-flowing fashion; there may not be time for punctuation or full sentences. Emojis and acronyms abound (LOL!), and extra punctuation is the norm (???!). Plus, there are various unwritten rules, such as avoiding ALL CAPS or periods at the end of a text. What's going on here?

The truth is that punctuation and grammar rules are not fixed. They are based on shared conventions, to help us communicate better, and these rules and niceties can change over time. Texts and online postings are quick, informal modes compared to written books and formal speech. Current punctuation usage reflects that trend.

Now, this loosey-goosey approach may cause grammar purists among us to grit their teeth. They may prefer correct punctuation in most cases. But following formal grammar rules in every setting, especially in casual ones, can send the wrong signal of its own. An old proverb says: "When in Rome, do as the Romans do." This saying means to follow the local practices of places you visit. This same approach applies to grammar. That is to say, when you're in a formal communication setting, by all means follow formal grammar rules. You'll be better understood and respected. In a casual setting, you can adapt and let the rules slide a bit, depending on your audience. This reduces friction and allows for a shared understanding, FWIW (for what it's worth). ☺

14

COMMA CORRAL
(AND PARENTHESES TOO)

Of all the punctuation marks, commas are the most challenging. They can be fussy and fleeting, optional and onerous. The main function of commas is to provide a slight pause in the text to clarify the meaning for readers (or as an aid in reading the text out loud). The pause created by commas is the shortest of all the punctuation marks, approximately a one-beat pause compared to a four-beat pause of a period or exclamation point (see the Musical-like Pauses of Punctuation chart on p 101).

Commas should enhance a reader's understanding, rather than interrupt the flow of words. The modern trend is to use fewer commas in sentences, so apply them carefully and with purpose—rather than randomly or inconsistently.

In general, use commas in the following instances:

1   **After introductory words and phrases:**

Furthermore, Muffin does not like to get her paws wet.

After a morning hike, we paddled our canoe to the donut shop.

Between gulps of water, Sam nervously practiced his speech.

2   **Between two or more adjectives before a noun if the order of the adjectives is interchangeable:**

It was a dark, stormy, bumpy pontoon ride.

Her rousing, snappy tap dance thrilled the audience.

A mysterious, odd-shaped letter arrived the next day.

TIP: If you can add the word *and* between the adjectives and it sounds ok, then use a comma between them. (See also p 67.)

3   **To separate three or more items in a series or list (words, phrases, or clauses) joined by *and* or *or*. This is called a serial or series comma.**

Unicycles, ukuleles, and umbrellas are on sale.

Big dogs, little dogs, cats, and mice all love cheese.

On the Fourth of July, we like to go swimming, eat hot dogs, and listen to the band playing in the park.

Note that some style guides omit the last comma in a list; however, adding the last comma prevents any confusion for readers. Consider the following example:

> Sophie was joined on stage by several good friends, a magician and a pet skunk.

In the example above, we don't know whether the magician and the skunk are Sophie's good friends, or additional friends joined the magician and skunk on the stage. An extra comma would clear it up.

4. **To set off direct addresses:**

> The immediate problem, dear friends, is that we're completely out of cat food.
>
> Bob, where are the keys to the broom closet?
>
> Would you like a saucer of cream, Tangi?

5. **For words, phrases, and clauses that are not essential to the sentence's meaning:**

> We were amazed, though not surprised, by Dr. Sullivan's giant pumpkins.
>
> His hasty explanation, however, was preposterous.
>
> Bowling, similar to golf, is both exhilarating and infuriating.
>
> Chloe, who loves smoked chicken, is my favorite cat.

TIP: If you can move the word or phrase anywhere in a sentence or remove it, and the sentence still makes sense, then it is *nonessential* and can be set off by commas.

6 **To set off appositives. Appositives are nouns (words or phrases) that further explain or stand in for another noun.**

Oliver, our black cat, is gazing intensely at the fish bowl.

Her feline assistant, Gazelle, greeted them at the door.

My birthday, August 30, is also National Toasted Marshmallow Day.

7 **Between two or more independent clauses joined by a conjunction such as *and, or, but, nor*:**

My orange tabby cat has lovely fur, and she matches the furniture beautifully.

You can bring your own didgeridoo, or you can purchase one at the gift shop.

TIP: An independent clause is a complete thought. It can stand on its own as a full sentence. Putting a comma followed by a conjunction between two independent clauses links them together and makes them sturdier.

TIP: For more about independent and dependent clauses, see Chapter 19.

8 **To separate a dependent clause (that often begins with words such as *although, because, since*, etc.) that comes before or after an independent clause:**

Since we left Cat's Creek, we haven't caught a single mouse.

Even though he took banjo lessons for six months, his playing still hadn't improved.

We attended the picnic, although it rained the whole time.

TIP: A dependent clause is not a complete thought. It's missing information for the reader and does not stand on its own as a full sentence. It is dependent on an independent clause to complete it.

9. **To set off nonessential (nonrestrictive) phrases or clauses:**

The old coat, which was falling apart, was his favorite.

His grumpy demeanor, as far as I can tell, started this afternoon.

The big cat, whose name we forgot, liked to steal flip flops and beach balls.

TIP: Nonessential phrases are not essential to the main meaning of a sentence. If you remove them, the sentence still makes sense.

10 **To set off quotes:**

She gasped, "Wow, that's a beautiful lake!"

Gandalf said, "I am looking for someone to share in an adventure that I am arranging, and it's very difficult to find anyone." (J. R. R. Tolkien, *The Hobbit*)

Pa asked, "Punctsie, have you seen any mice today?"

"Oh, that is a rather useful dragon-detecting device," he replied.

11 **After digits in numbers that denote thousands, millions, billions, and trillions:**

$1,000 $10,000 $10,000,000

   $10,000,000,000 $10,000,000,000,000

12 **In addresses (streets, cities, states, and countries) and dates:**

She lives in Missoula, Montana, and studies grizzly bears.

On April 24, 1990, the Hubble telescope was launched into orbit.

13 **Do not use a comma between a verb and a subject, object, or subject complement.** A subject complement more fully describes, explains, or renames a subject.

Incorrect: The drive-in movie, was exciting.

Correct: The drive-in movie was exciting.

Incorrect: The superheroes include, Blue Beetle and Ant-Man.

Correct: The superheroes include Blue Beetle and Ant-Man.

TIP: Watch for commas that interrupt the flow of the sentence. These stray commas are a bit like littering the road with an old tire that your readers may stumble over.

14 **Avoid putting commas between two independent clauses without using a conjunction (*and, but, or,* etc.). This creates a run-on sentence (aka a comma splice).**

Incorrect: Cats are crepuscular creatures, they are active at dusk and dawn.

Fix this type of error by (1) adding a conjunction after the comma, (2) adding a semicolon between the two clauses, (3) creating two separate sentences, or (4) changing one of the independent clauses to a dependent clause, as follows.

Correct: Cats are crepuscular creatures, so they are active at dusk and dawn.

Correct: Cats are crepuscular creatures; they are active at dusk and dawn.

Correct: Cats are crepuscular creatures. They are active at dusk and dawn.

Correct: Cats are crepuscular creatures, which means they are active at dusk and dawn.

15 **Avoid oddly placed or random commas. These stray commas may confuse or distract readers.**

Incorrect: Although, he liked banana ice cream, the shop had only strawberry.

Correct: Although he liked banana ice cream, the shop had only strawberry.

Incorrect: Rollerblading, biking and, ice-skating are fun.

Correct: Rollerblading, biking, and ice-skating are fun.

ANIMALS CREPUSCULAR

We like twilight animals crepuscular,
Who come out at dawn and at duskular.
Their game is to eat
But not be the meat,
Of predators greatly more muscular.

Those wonderful animals crepuscular
Can sometimes be very "fusscular."
Like skunks, moose, and cats,
Hyenas and rats,
And warthogs that are seriously tuskular!

—*Don Hart*

IN PARENTHESES

Parentheses are the funky cousins of commas. They can act like commas sometimes, but they have their own style and usage.

Most cats love a parenthesis (plural: parentheses). It reminds them of encircling a trapped mouse. That's because parentheses set off a word, clause, or sentence as a further explanation (or an afterthought). A parenthesis doesn't remind you of encircling a mouse? Then you are not a cat.

A main sentence is complete without parentheses. However, words inside the parentheses tell more about what has already been said. For example,

Punctsie has four kittens (Coo, Gemma, Maggie, and Susie Q).

As a parent cat, Punctsie curves her front paws to hold her kittens next to her while she licks them. Her arms are like parentheses. When you use parentheses in a sentence, remember you are holding words that go together—to further explain something or to add a side comment.

Punctsie's favorite thing to write in parentheses is her explanation of what *really* happens when we see her make a big mistake (which she meant to do). Examples from her diary:

When I coughed up a big hairball in front of my bridal shower guests, most of them didn't understand. (I meant to do that.)

On Saturday, I knocked over a plate of chocolate cupcakes at a birthday party, and all the children began screaming. (I meant to do that.)

Notice that parentheses are always used in pairs. Also, when parentheses are used around a complete sentence, the punctuation goes *inside* the last parenthesis. (That means no punctuation mark is left out!)

15

ALL ABOUT APOSTROPHES

Oliver's cat toy

Oliver's clever!

Even though apostrophes are little marks that might be overlooked, they can have big power in sentences. Apostrophes are used in two main ways: contractions and possessives.

APOSTROPHES AND CONTRACTIONS

When an apostrophe works as a contraction, it represents missing letters, such as in the word *you'll*. Of course, *you'll* is a contraction for *you will*. Here are some other examples:

She'll go in the afternoon.	She will go in the afternoon.
They're smart people.	They are smart people.

I've never traded a horse.   I have never traded a horse.

Sometimes writers use contractions in dialogue to give their writing a more folksy, regional, or down-to-earth style, which is the way some people talk.

Y'all come from Texas?   You all come from Texas?

That car ain't worth nothin'.   That car is not worth anything.

He'da gone fishin' if it wasn't rainin'.   He would have gone fishing if it was not raining.

Contractions are mainly used in informal writing. When you are writing more formally on a serious topic, it's generally not a good idea to use them.

APOSTROPHES AND POSSESSIVES

Besides being used to form contractions, apostrophes are also used to create the possessive form for many words. For example, apostrophes are used for possessive nouns to indicate ownership. These are fairly simple, especially if the noun is singular. In these cases, the noun is followed by apostrophe + s. For example,

Steve's cat is cuddly.

Steve's cat's toys are missing.

It's still straightforward when the possessive noun is plural as in

My cats' toys are great fun (even for me)!

My six cats' 36 kittens are all black and white.

Our next writers' meeting will feature a screenwriter and a jingle writer.

However, apostrophes and possessive nouns can sometimes cause confusion. One example you will want to know well is the word *its*. *Its* is a possessive term that means the property of whatever you are writing about, for example,

The book has lost its cover.

Its title is too long.

Notice that an apostrophe does not appear in the word "its" used in a possessive sense in the sentences above. "It's" (which uses an apostrophe) is a contraction and means *it is*.

It's time for dessert.

We think it's sad to have run out of cake.

APOSTROPHES FOR DATES, LETTERS, AND NUMBERS

Apostrophes are generally not used in the plurals of full dates, letters, and numbers. For example,

In the 1860s, hot air balloon military spying was all the rage.

Andrew's secret password has many Ls and 9s and two 7s.

However, an apostrophe + s may be used for plurals of letters or numbers, if adding just an s would make the term confusing.

I have to mind my p's and q's when visiting the royal dining room.

His bingo card had no I's filled in.

This code contains 1's and 0's.

(Note that without the added apostrophes in the sentences above, ps, Is, and 1s could be mistaken for words rather than plurals.)

Apostrophes are normally not used for plural forms of words:

Incorrect: She likes banana's and apple's.
Correct: She likes bananas and apples.

Incorrect: There are many Smith's in my history class.
Correct: There are many Smiths in my history class.

Apostrophes are used to indicate missing numbers in decades and for possessives of numbers and letters.

Meghan likes the teal kitchen designs from the '50s.

The Model T's engine generated 20 horsepower and a fair bit of rattling.

For more about using apostrophes with possessives, see Chapter 18: Possessives (or Don't Touch My Paws).

16

MAD DASHES
AND HYPHEN HYPE

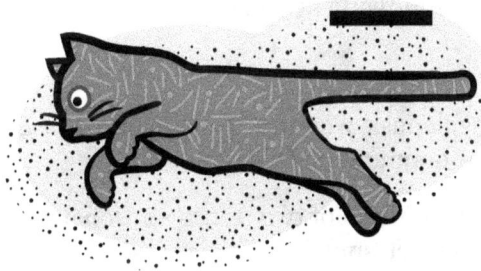

D ashes are very useful for writers because they are punctuation that you never *have* to use, but you may find them very handy anyway. They can add a bit of dazzle and flash to writing. Just be careful not to overdo them. There are two kinds of dashes, the M dash and the N dash. Let's see what each one can do.

THE M DASH (—) (THE MAD DASH)

M dashes (—) are different than N dashes (–). M dashes are slightly longer and a bit more fun than N dashes, and they are as wide as the letter M. Think of M dashes as the long, mad dashes that cats make when they are chasing a mouse.

The M dash can be a substitute for other punctuation marks such as commas, parentheses, or colons. As such, they can create a short or long pause depending on the context. When you use M dashes, you make the words following them more forceful, dramatic, or emphatic than normal. Hence, M dashes must be used in moderation, or they will begin to wear out their welcome. This would be like knowing a man with a loud, stentorian voice. The first time or two you heard him speak, he would sound very impressive, but if he continued talking like Winston Churchill warning Parliament of the awful coming World War, you'd soon tire of the guy. All in all, M dashes are great if they are used skillfully in places where your writing needs a bit of drama and style.

Using M dashes instead of colons. Colons are more formal than M dashes. However, because of their appearance, M dashes can be more emphatic than colons. When you want to inject stronger feeling into your writing, use M dashes instead of colons. Compare the impact of the following sentences.

> Our cat, Snagglepuss, was afraid of two things: a Doberman Pinscher next door and black spiders.
>
> Snagglepuss was afraid of two things—a Doberman Pinscher next door and black spiders.

See how the M dash is a bit more noticeable and dramatic compared to a colon? However, it may all come down to personal preference.

Using M dashes instead of semicolons, commas, or parentheses. M dashes can be used in place of semicolons, commas, or parentheses when you want to add a bit of flair to your sentences.

> Courage is the greatest virtue;
> it always has been.
>
> Courage is the greatest virtue
> —it always has been.

The greatest virtue (courage) is needed for sustaining other virtues.

The greatest virtue, courage, is needed for sustaining other virtues.

The greatest virtue—courage—is needed for sustaining other virtues.

THE N DASH (–) (THE NEIGHBORLY DASH)

The N dash is a punctuation mark that looks similar to the hyphen and minus sign, but it's slightly longer and differs from these symbols in meaning. Think of N dashes as short, friendly dashes that cats make when they scamper to meet their neighbor. N dashes are used to join similar types of words (pairs, for instance). They are also used in numerical ranges, which makes them quite neighborly. Here are some examples.

1 **Use the N dash to denote spans of time or ranges of numbers.**

My cat is available for an appointment with me on Wednesday at 12–12:30 p.m. when she is not napping.

Puddy normally chases 6–10 mice every day.

2 **Use N dashes between equivalent words or phrases.**

North–South connection

acid–base solution

salmon–chicken entree

HYPHEN HYPE

A hyphen is used to join words in a way that gives them a new meaning when used together. An example is "He wore his brother's hand-me-down clothes." Another use for hyphens is to separate syllables in a word, which is done to show breaks at the end of a sentence. You can also use hyphens when you want to connect several words together to describe something more descriptive than normal.

My cat-show-winning feline seemed pleased to have me escort her onto the stage.

My first cat disliked stay-at-home mice and hairballs.

Note that a minus sign should never be confused with hyphens or N dashes. The minus sign is a mathematical symbol used in subtraction. A minus sign is slightly thinner and has a length somewhere between a hyphen and an N dash. Check instructions for your software to discover quick keystrokes to create M dashes, N dashes, and minus signs on your electronic device.

For much more information about hyphen use, see Chapter 25: Consistency Cat-isthentics.

17

QUOTE-UNQUOTE

" It was a dark and stormy night... "

Quotation marks (" ") are sometimes called quote marks or speech marks. They are always used in pairs. They are mainly used to set off the text where someone's speech is being quoted, such as an unusual sentence, word, or phrase.

Terry Pratchett said, "In ancient times cats were worshipped as gods; they have not forgotten this."

Mark Twain said, "When a man loves cats, I am his friend and comrade, without further introduction."

Mary Bly wrote, "Dogs come when they're called; cats take a message and get back to you later."

Another useful purpose of quotation marks is for indicating titles. Italics, quotation marks, and underlining are all used for titles. Books and movies would normally be italicized or underlined, depending on the style used. The main rule, though, is that quotation marks are used especially for short works: poetry, short stories, and chapter titles.

"Animals Crepuscular" is a great limerick poem. (See p 118.)

My favorite short story is "The Day I Killed Henry," about a small boy whose life was threatened by a gander.

A romantic war movie, starring Humphrey Bogart, is *Casablanca*.

DIRECT VERSUS INDIRECT QUOTES

Quotes come in several varieties: direct and indirect. When you use a direct quote, you are indicating exactly what a person or character said. When doing this, always use quotation marks. When your quotes are indirect, meaning not a person's direct speech, you do not need quotes because you are summarizing or paraphrasing what someone said.

Direct quote: Ryan said, "My cat doesn't mind a bath, but he insists on a bubble bath."

Indirect quote: Ryan told me his cat likes bubble baths.

Direct quote: "Nephelococcygia is seeking and finding familiar shapes in clouds. It is becoming a popular hobby," said the meteorologist.

Indirect quote: The meteorologist said that cloud gazing is a fun and popular hobby.

In American English, the general rule is to keep commas and periods inside the quotation marks. Other punctuation marks (semicolons, dashes, colons, question marks, and exclamation marks) may go inside or outside of the quotation marks, depending on the usage. A good rule of thumb is to put punctuation marks inside quotes if they apply to the quote only. Put them outside of the quote marks if they apply to the whole sentence. For example,

"The smallest feline," said Leonardo da Vinci, "is a masterpiece."

"A cat has absolute emotional honesty: human beings, for one reason or another, may hide their feelings," said Ernest Hemingway, "but a cat does not."

SEMIQUOTATIONS

Semiquotes (also called single quotes) are quotes that appear inside another quote. This type of quote is punctuated by single quotation marks (' ') and is used inside a quote to display a quote by another person. The placement of punctuation marks inside or outside of the quote marks depends on whether it's part of the original quotation or not. For example,

The reporter asked, "What did you mean when you said 'unintended consequences'?"

She exclaimed, "I agree with Henry James when he said, 'You can learn more about a person in an hour of play than in a month of conversation.'"

USING QUOTE MARKS AROUND A WORD OR PHRASE

When writers use quote marks around a word or phrase, they are usually pointing out an irony, humor, or level of distrust about a term or phrase being used. Often, the quotes warn the reader of a coming contradiction or figure of speech. They provide commentary, which could be humorous or biting.

Frito is an "inside cat" but constantly wants to go outside, unless he is currently outside (in which case, he wants to go inside).

Morris, our neighborhood tomcat, met a new "frenemy" cat named Edward who decided, perhaps unwisely, to visit Morris's yard.

Quote marks can be a forewarning that the writer thinks a term is perhaps misleading or phony. They can also be used for newly invented terms or to signal to readers that there is a spoof at play or something is amiss. For instance, if you see quotes around terms such as "new" or "improved," you may wonder if they are really new and improved, or the writer isn't so sure. Using these kinds of quotes can be easily misunderstood by readers and can be overused, especially in editorial writing or political essays. So, be thoughtful about quotation marks around terms because they may be confusing to some readers. To quote writer David McCullough: "Writing is thinking. To write well is to think clearly. That's why it's so hard."

Punctuation Personality Awards

SEMICOLON (;)
Hoity Toity, but Useful

EXCLAMATION POINT (!)
Drama Queen

QUOTATION MARK (")
Tattle Teller

COMMA (,)
Most Ambitious

Honorable Mentions

Period: Most likely to succeed

Question Mark: Poignant, at times rhetorical

Dash: Abrupt, but dapper

Hyphen: Word matchmaker, though a bit flaky

Apostrophe: Most misunderstood, somewhat possessive

Parentheses: Generous, inclusive, though
sometimes beside the point

Colon: Show-off

Ellipsis: Most understated

SECTION 3
AVOIDING GRAMMAR CATASTROPHES

18

POSSESSIVES
(OR DON'T TOUCH MY PAWS)

YOURS

MINE

Possessives are words that show ownership. This concept is clear to cats. For instance, you may think a certain chair is *yours*. You are mistaken. The chair is actually the cat's new napping spot. Possibly you think the couch is yours too. Silly you. It's actually *his* scratching post. And *your* window is, truth be told, the cat's TV. By the way, *your* hot dog could suddenly become *their* hot dog if the cats decide to steal a bite.

Although possessive forms are obvious to cats, they can sometimes cause confusion. However, possessives are straightforward and fun if you know a few basic rules about them. First, nouns and pronouns have possessive forms. *Possessive nouns* can be singular (cat's,

Betty's) or plural (kittens', mice's). They include proper nouns and names, people, places, and things. *Possessive pronouns* can act in place of a noun (*mine, ours, theirs*) or as adjectives (*my, our, their*).

Before we move on, let's review apostrophes. You learned in Chapter 15 (All About Apostrophes) that apostrophes serve several purposes: forming contractions and showing possession of things. For contractions, apostrophes indicate missing letters in a word. For possessives, apostrophes indicate ownership (for example, for possessive nouns such as "Jill's flowers").

Contraction: He's my favorite tomcat.

Contraction: I'd like to attend the cat show in Muncie.

Possessive: The cats' boxing match lasted four rounds.

Possessive: Rayce did a quick inventory of his cat's toys and her kittens' mittens.

Combination of a possessive and a contraction: Archibald loves Shakespeare's play *Love's Labor's Lost.*

RULES FOR POSSESSIVE NOUNS

As we mentioned, possessive nouns show ownership for people, places, and things. The possessive nouns use apostrophes to indicate ownership. The apostrophe looks a bit like a cat using her claw to grab onto something she wants. When forming possessive nouns, it's important to pay attention to whether the noun is singular or plural and whether it ends in -s or -z or something else. Here are some basic rules for creating the possessive forms of nouns and names.

1. **For singular nouns and names that don't end in -s, add apostrophe + -s ('s) to the end of the noun or name.**

The kitten's mittens were purchased at Catmart.

Leroy's brown cat is named Cocoa.

In her mind's eye, she created a new gadget.

The town's claim to fame is its Mustard Museum.

We did not know that the old gray mare was Don's.

THE CLOWN'S BOUNCE

Add apostrophe S
To a singular noun,
And learn to bounce
From a springular clown.

2. **For singular nouns and names that end in -s or -z, add an apostrophe + -s ('s) or just an apostrophe to the end of the noun to create the possessive form.** Note this rule varies depending on the style guide (*The Chicago Manual of Style, The Associated Press Stylebook*, etc.). Consult whichever one you're following and be consistent.

Chris's chair or Chris' chair

the boss's schedule or the boss' schedule

Santa Cruz's soccer league or Santa Cruz' soccer league.

⟵ **TIP**: For classical or religious names ending in -s or -z, the accepted practice is to add only an apostrophe after the name for the possessive.

Socrates' writings

Theophilus' book

THE TENNESSEE WALTZ'S RHYTHM

For one dancing noun or a name
Ending in S or Z
To the end of that word
Slide in an apostrophe S or an apostrophe

3 For plural nouns not ending in -s or -z, add apostrophe + -s ('s) to the end of the noun.

children's books

women's trip

men's shirts

mice's cheese

THE OXEN'S REVENGE

For any plural noun
Not ending in Z or S,
Add apostrophe S to its ending
To avoid any stress.

4. **For plural nouns and names that end in -s, add an apostrophe to the end of the noun.**

the kittens' mittens

the dogs' bowls

the Rosses' camper

TIP: For the possessive form of names that end in -s, create the plural form of the name first. Then, add an apostrophe to the end of the name.

the Combses' holiday card

the Petrillas' mailbox

OUR CATS' FAVORITE TOY

Use S, then Apostrophe,
For a noun that is plural;
And buy Slinkies with feathers
In the shape of a squirrel.

5. **For compound nouns that jointly possess something, add 's to the last noun only. For compound nouns that own something separately, add 's to the end of each noun.**

Tiny and Biggy's house (one house)

Tiny's and Biggy's houses (separate houses)

6 **Use 's with time periods.**

this year's events

today's profits

yesterday's news

POSSESSIVE PRONOUNS

Pronouns stand in for nouns. Like possessive nouns, pronouns can show ownership by people, places, and things using the possessive form. A *possessive pronoun* replaces the noun it refers to. For example,

That fancy hat is *mine*.

We thought the painting was *hers*.

The final decision is *yours*.

The black pony is *ours*.

Note that possessive pronouns don't use apostrophes. However, some of them use an -s at the end of the word.

POSSESSIVE PRONOUNS

hers	its	ours	yours (singular and plural)
his	mine	theirs	

POSSESSIVE ADJECTIVES

Possessive adjectives describe nouns rather than replace them. They also show ownership and indicate which noun they are describing.

My favorite chair is taken.

We followed *our* cousin to *his* house.

The flower opened *its* petals.

POSSESSIVE ADJECTIVES

her	its	our	your (singular and plural)
his	my	their	

TIP: The word *its* is possessive. This is not to be confused with the contraction it's meaning *it is*. By the way, there is no such word as its', so don't use it.

Remember: Don't use apostrophes with possessive pronouns (*his, hers, its, theirs, yours, ours*) and possessive adjectives (*its, his*). This is grammatically incorrect, not to mention confusing. Use apostrophes for possessive nouns and names only.

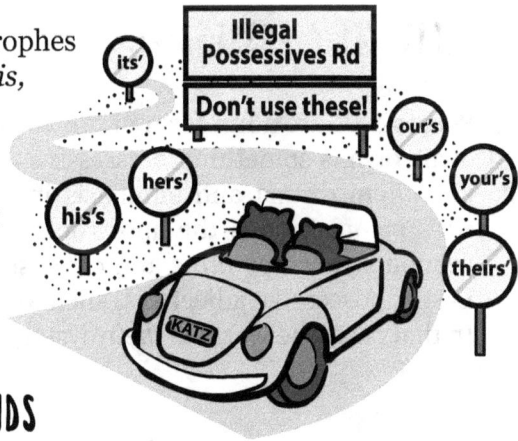

Illegal Possessives Rd

Don't use these!

its' our's hers' your's his's theirs'

KATZ

POSSESSIVES AND GERUNDS

Gerunds are nouns that end in -ing. Possessive adjectives can be used with gerunds. For example,

<u>Her whistling</u> during the song was distracting. (*Her* indicates which whistling.)

I loved <u>his dancing</u> in the movie. (*His* indicates which dancing.)

WHY WOULDN'T YOU PAY FOR APOSTROPHES?

If you had to pay for an apostrophe
Any cost would be an "imposterfee,"
Like charging a cat for her strokes,
Would become a terrible hoax
Soon considered a complete "preposterfee"!

But Possessives are so very tricky
That your grammar needs to be picky.
So paying where to place that apostrophe
Should involve an extra "coststostrofee"
And your writing will never get sticky.

—*Don Hart*

POSITIVELY POSSESSIVE

Possessives are a fun form of nouns and pronouns. They show who owns or has something. Possessive nouns use apostrophes, which give them drama and emphasis in a sentence. They are like the *cat's meow* (notice the apostrophe in "cat's meow"?). Possessive pronouns, such as *mine* and *ours*, stand in for a possessive noun. Lastly, possessive adjectives, such as *my* and *her*, describe a noun. In that case, the world is *their* oyster, too.

19

INDEPENDENT AND DEPENDENT CLAUSES ("CLAWSES")

C ats are independent creatures. This means you can bake a special cake for your cat complete with salmon mousse frosting and candles. But when you try to sing happy birthday to her and offer her a piece of cake, she may prefer to sit in the window and growl-purr at chipmunks instead. She's an independent cat who likes to stand on her own.

Dogs, on the other hand, are more dependent. They like to follow you around the house all day, sit in your lap even though they are too big, and play fetch for hours until you finally hide the toy. Dogs, generally speaking, are dependent creatures who like to be near someone all the time.

The independent nature of cats and the dependent nature of dogs help us understand independent and dependent clauses. How is that? First of all, what is a clause? (If you have a cat or dog, you already know what *claws* are.) A *clause* is a group of words that has a subject and a verb. There are two types of clauses: *independent clauses* and *dependent clauses*. Let's review each one.

INDEPENDENTLY MINDED CLAUSES

An independent clause is a complete thought with a subject and a verb. It can stand on its own as a complete sentence. For example,

A bag of cat treats sits on the counter.

This is an independent clause and also a complete sentence. We can combine two independent clauses to build a story. When we do this, we separate the two independent clauses with one of the following:

- 🐾 a period (as two separate sentences)
- 🐾 a semicolon
- 🐾 a comma + coordinating conjunction (*and, or, but*, etc.).

For example,

A bag of cat treats sits on the counter. I don't think it will last long there. (two independent clauses as separate sentences)

A bag of cat treats sits on the counter; I don't think it will last long there. (two independent clauses separated by a semicolon)

A bag of cat treats sits on the counter, but I don't think it will last long there. (two independent clauses separated by a comma and the conjunction *but*)

Independent clauses stand tall on their own, like a cat does. They stand out in writing for their strength of thought. Correct punctuation around independent clauses is important. For example,

- Use a period after each independent clause, which allows them to stand firmly on their own as separate sentences.

- Use a semicolon between them if they are closely related sentences.

- Use a comma and coordinating conjunction (*and, but, or, for, nor, yet, so*) between them if they are related in a particular way, as specified by the conjunction (see Chapter 10).

Avoid running two independent clauses together using only commas. This creates a run-on sentence and prevents the independent clauses from standing independently. Instead, they are muddled together, like cats running over each other. Independent clauses, like cats, don't like to be run together with another independent clause. Separate them with the proper punctuation.

Incorrect: The sky was full of stars, the moon was shining.

Correct: The sky was full of stars. The moon was shining.

Correct: The sky was full of stars; the moon was shining.

Correct: The sky was full of stars, and the moon was shining.

More than two independent clauses can occur in one sentence. In this case, each clause is separated by a comma, with a comma + conjunction added before the last independent clause, creating a more complex sentence.

Paul has a pet rabbit, Greta has two geckos, and I have a black snake.

Notice commas set off each independent clause above. This is not only grammatically correct, but also it strengthens writing by showing readers where each complete thought ends and makes the meaning clearer.

PUNCTUATION FOR TWO INDEPENDENT CLAUSES

The excited cat ran up the tree. She had trouble getting down.

The excited cat ran up the tree; she had trouble getting down.

The excited cat ran up the tree, but she had trouble getting down.

SIGNAL WORDS FOR INDEPENDENT CLAUSES

Certain words show relationships between independent clauses. These words include *thus, therefore, namely, furthermore, indeed,* and *conversely.* They are called *conjunctive adverbs.* They help sentences flow by providing a smooth transition from one independent clause to the next (see a complete list of these words in the chart on p 150). They show time, order, contrast, consequence of events, additions, and added emphasis. (See Chapter 10, pp 85-87.)

Conjunctive adverbs sound good to the ear and give sentences crispness and precision. They also signal that the clause that follows a conjunctive adverb may be an independent clause if it's a complete sentence. So, it's useful to remember these words so you'll know how to punctuate your sentences correctly.

Note that conjunctive adverbs are *adverbs,* not conjunctions. Conjunctive adverbs show relationships between two independent clauses rather than join sentences like coordinating conjunctions do. If you use a conjunctive adverb, look to see if what follows it is an independent clause. If so, use a semicolon or a period between the two independent clauses, as shown below.

He accidentally broke the lamp; <u>however</u>, it was not his favorite.

It was a frigid, snowy day. <u>Consequently</u>, we wore our heavy winter coats.

A spider ran out of sight under the cabinet; <u>nevertheless</u>, the cat watched for it all day.

TIP: Conjunctive adverbs can be moved around in a sentence, and it still makes sense. Note that a comma is usually used after a conjunctive adverb if it appears at the beginning of an independent clause.

A conjunctive adverb appears between the two independent clauses in the examples above. A semicolon or a period is used between the clauses. If you use a comma instead, it creates a run-on sentence (also called a comma splice).

Incorrect: I wanted to wear my favorite sweater to the party, however, one of the buttons was missing.

Correct: I wanted to wear my favorite sweater to the party; however, one of the buttons was missing.

Correct: I wanted to wear my favorite sweater to the party. However, one of the buttons was missing.

Keeping a list of conjunctive adverbs handy will help you know how to properly punctuate sentences containing two independent clauses. When you see one of these "signal" words, check to see if an independent clause follows it. If so, use a period or a semicolon to connect the two independent clauses.

CONJUNCTIVE ADVERBS

accordingly	further	nevertheless	thereafter
additionally	furthermore	next	therefore
again	hence	nonetheless	thus
also	henceforth	now	ultimately
alternatively	however	of course	undoubtedly
anyway	in addition	on the other hand	
as a result	incidentally	otherwise	
as such	in conclusion	overall	
besides	in contrast	rather	
certainly	indeed	regardless	
consequently	in fact	similarly	
conversely	in particular	so (when it means "thus")	
elsewhere	instead		
eventually	later	specifically	
finally	likewise	still	
first	meanwhile	subsequently	
for example	moreover	that is	
for instance	namely	then	

DEPENDENT (BUT HAPPY) CLAUSES

Dependent clauses (also called *subordinate clauses*) have a subject and a verb, but unlike independent clauses, they are not complete thoughts by themselves. Dependent clauses cannot stand on their own. They don't make sense by themselves. They need an independent clause to provide more information to complete the sentence. Below are some dependent clauses.

When I saw the prize-winning goats

Although taking a boat was faster

Notice the above clauses are not complete thoughts. Some crucial information is missing. As readers, we are left hanging, waiting for more, like a dog dragging a leash. Let's complete the thought by adding an independent clause to it. For instance,

When I saw the prize-winning goats, I congratulated my friend.

Although taking a boat was faster, we took the train instead.

In the above sentences, we have a dependent clause followed by an independent clause, which creates a complete sentence. Dependent clauses support independent clauses by adding additional information to the sentence. Dependent clauses can appear before or after an independent clause. If a dependent clause comes before an independent clause, it is usually separated by a comma. If the dependent clause comes after an independent clause, a comma is often not used. However, in some cases a comma is used to help clarify the meaning. Below are some examples (dependent clauses are underlined).

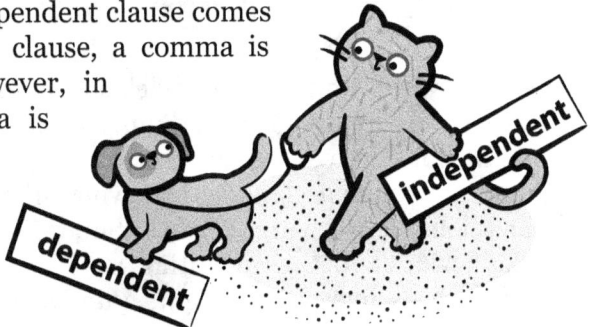

By the time we found the flower shop, it was already closed.

If you finish your dinner, you'll get a treat.

We headed home from the game because it was getting dark.

The hike was treacherous, although the mountain views were spectacular.

Linda cleans the house, while Fluffy eats from the butter dish left on the kitchen counter.

PLACEMENT OF DEPENDENT CLAUSES

BEFORE

When we rang the doorbell, a poodle ran to the door.

AFTER

A poodle ran to the door when we rang the doorbell.

LINKING WORDS FOR DEPENDENT AND INDEPENDENT CLAUSES

Certain words link dependent clauses and independent clauses. These words are called *subordinating conjunctions*. Subordinating conjunctions are very useful words to help join a dependent clause to an independent clause by showing different relationships and transitions between the clauses. Subordinating conjunctions are linking words that give writing style and sophistication. These useful words include *although, after, because*, and *even though* (see a full list of subordinating conjunctions in the chart on p 154).

As soon as we heard the sirens, we braced for the storm.

I can make a dessert from scratch provided that I have chocolate chips and peanut butter.

Even though the house was spooky, we wanted to walk by it.

Notice that if a subordinating conjunction occurs at the beginning of a clause, *it automatically makes that clause a dependent clause*. In other words, a subordinating conjunction can turn an independent clause into a dependent clause. A separate independent clause is then needed to complete the sentence.

Our group won the camp talent show.
(independent clause, complete sentence)

Although our group won the camp talent show (dependent clause, needs an independent clause to complete the sentence)

Although our group won the camp talent show, we lost the knot tying competition.
(dependent clause with an independent clause added; complete sentence)

Subordinating conjunctions are useful words to remember because they signal a dependent clause may follow, and this helps you punctuate sentences correctly. Subordinating conjunctions also help sentences flow because they link dependent and independent clauses together smoothly. Instead of seeing a string of sentences with no real connections, readers can see the different relationships between clauses, such as time (*when, before, after*), specific conditions (*as long as, if*), or contrasts (*although, whereas*).

Note that *whereas, because,* and *although* are not conjunctive adverbs that we discussed earlier. Rather, these are *subordinating conjunctions* that begin a dependent clause. Don't use semicolons to separate independent and dependent clauses, which will create a fragment. Instead, use commas to set off the dependent clause.

Incorrect: Willis liked to visit the rose park; even though, it made him sneeze.

Correct: Willis liked to visit the rose park, even though it made him sneeze.

SUBORDINATING CONJUNCTIONS

after	how	that	whereas
although	if	though	wherever
as	inasmuch as	till	whether
as if	just as	unless	which
as long as	now	until	whichever
as much as	now that	whatever	while
as soon as	once	when	who
assuming that	only if	whenever	whoever
as though	provided	where	whom
because	provided that		whomever
before	rather than		
by the time	since		
even if	so that		
even though	than		

TYPES OF DEPENDENT CLAUSES

Dependent clauses can function in various ways in a sentence: as adverbs, adjectives, or nouns. Let's look at some examples.

Dependent clauses as adverbs. When they function as adverbs, dependent clauses modify a verb and answer the question *when, how, how often, where, to what degree, under what conditions,* and *why* in a sentence. For example,

> He feels happy <u>when he sings</u>. (answers *when*)
>
> We saw purple flowers <u>wherever we looked</u>. (answers *where*)
>
> <u>Because I put off writing my essay</u>, I have to work on it this weekend. (answers *why*)
>
> I'll ride my bike <u>if it's sunny tomorrow</u>. (answers *under what conditions*)

TIP: Dependent adverb clauses can usually be put at the beginning or end of the sentence, and the sentence will still make sense.

Dependent clauses as nouns. Dependent clauses can also act as nouns in a sentence. Just like nouns, they can act as a subject, direct object, indirect object, object of a preposition, or subject complement. These types of clauses usually start with *who, whoever, whom, whomever, that, which, when, where,* and *whose.* Unlike adverb dependent clauses, noun dependent clauses cannot be moved around in the sentence.

> We noticed <u>that a cow was standing in the road</u>. (acts as a direct object, indicating what we saw)
>
> <u>Whoever drank all the chocolate milk</u> should replace it. (acts as the subject)
>
> I am thankful for <u>whatever advice you can give me</u>. (acts as the object of a preposition)

Dependent clauses as adjectives. Dependent clauses can also function as adjectives to describe or modify a noun or pronoun. These clauses usually start with a relative pronoun such as *who, whoever, whom, whomever, that, which, when, where*, and *whose*. These clauses answer the question *which one, which kind*, or *who*.

Keisha, <u>who usually feeds the class bunny</u>, is absent today.

The electric bike <u>that I drive</u> gets excellent gas mileage.

Lichun's Hawaiian farm, <u>which has bananas</u>, is near the ocean.

Essential versus nonessential dependent clauses. You'll notice in the above sentences that some dependent clauses are set off by commas and some are not. The difference is that some clauses are *essential* and others are *nonessential*. These types of clauses are also called *restrictive* and *nonrestrictive,* respectively.

Essential (or restrictive) clauses are necessary to understand the main meaning of the sentence, whereas nonessential (or nonrestrictive) clauses are not necessary to the meaning of the sentence. Nonessential clauses provide additional information as an aside. However, they can be omitted without changing the overall meaning of the sentence.

Nonessential clauses are usually set off by commas, parentheses, or dashes to show they are not critical to the sentence's meaning. You can easily pluck these clauses out, and the sentence will still make sense. Essential clauses, in contrast, are not set off by commas or other punctuation. In other words, they are strongly embedded in the sentence's meaning. If you omit an essential clause, the remaining sentence is unclear. The absence or presence of punctuation around clauses helps readers know whether a clause is essential or nonessential to the sentence. For instance,

The electric bike <u>that I drive</u> gets excellent gas mileage. (This clause is essential; it specifies a particular bike, the one I drive.)

My electric bike, <u>which I drive every day</u>, gets excellent gas mileage. (This clause, set off by commas, is nonessential; it gives additional information but could be omitted.)

The curtains <u>that have hung in the hall for years</u> were very dusty. (This clause is essential; it specifies which curtains, the ones in the hall.)

The curtains—<u>which we hung outside</u>— were very dusty. (This clause, set off by dashes, is nonessential; it provides additional information.)

Note that the writer can change a sentence's meaning simply by adding or not adding commas around a dependent clause. Here's an example:

The tourists who took the bus missed seeing the bear.

(This clause is essential because it is not set off by commas; it specifies that these particular tourists, the ones who took the bus, missed the bear. Maybe the tourists who hiked saw it!)

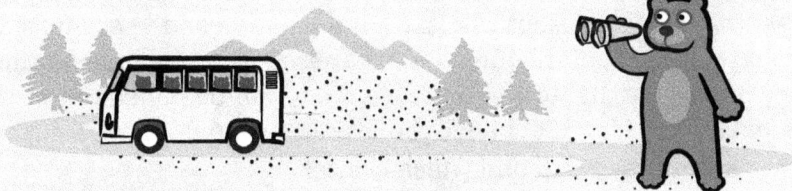

The tourists, who took the bus, missed seeing the bear.

(This clause is nonessential because it is set off by commas; it gives additional information about the tourists, all of whom missed seeing the bear.)

TIP: If a dependent clause can be left out of the sentence, and it still makes sense, the clause is nonessential and should be separated by commas (or parentheses or dashes).

Be thoughtful about placing commas around dependent clauses so readers can understand your meaning. If the information in the clause is essential, omit commas. If the information is extra or a side comment, add the commas.

That versus which in dependent clauses. *That* and *which* are commonly found at the beginning of dependent clauses. Many people think you can use that and which interchangeably or randomly. However, grammatically speaking, their meanings are somewhat different. The general rule is to use *that* when you want to indicate that the information is *essential* to the meaning of the sentence. In other words, the clause is embedded in the sentence's meaning. If you remove a clause starting with *that*, the sentence would not make sense or would not be clear.

One way to remember *that* is essential is to think of the T in *that* as a piece of Toast. Toast is essential—or at least many people around the world consider toast (or some bread version of it) an essential food!

THAT IS ESSENTIAL

Which can be used for essential or nonessential clauses. However, *which* is more often used for nonessential clauses to indicate the information is not essential to the meaning of the sentence. In this case, the *which* clause is just extra information added as an aside. *Which* clauses that are nonessential are set off by commas to show they are not crucial to the sentence. They can be pulled out of the sentence, and it won't change the overall meaning. Here are some other examples of that and which clauses.

The model plane <u>that we built</u> flew 100 yards.

(The clause *that we built* is essential; it specifies a particular plane, the one we built. Note that commas are omitted.)

Our model plane, <u>which flew only 10 yards</u>, crashed into the field.

(The clause *which flew only 10 yards* is nonessential because it is set off by commas; it just provides additional information but could be omitted.)

Commas are used to create nonessential *which* "sandwiches." These *which* clauses are sandwiched between two commas if the clause is in the middle of the sentence or between a comma and a period if the clause is at the end of a sentence. Commas signal to readers that the clause is nonessential.

USE A WHICH SANDWICH FOR NONESSENTIAL CLAUSES

WHICH

comma–comma
sandwich

The canoe, which we rented, was red.

comma–period
sandwich

We rented the last canoe, which was red.

Now let's see how using a "which" sandwich instead of "that" can change a sentence's meaning.

She won the marathon that was held in Cincinnati.

(The clause is essential because it uses *that* and is not set off by commas; it specifies which marathon she won, the one in Cincinnati, as opposed to another city.)

She won the marathon, which was held in Cincinnati.

(The clause is nonessential because of the added comma; the important fact is she won the marathon; as an aside, we are told where it was held.)

BUILDING BETTER SENTENCES WITH CLAUSES

Independent and dependent clauses are the basic building blocks of sentences. You can tie independent and dependent clauses together to build more complex thoughts and ideas. Linking words, such as coordinating conjunctions, conjunctive adverbs, and subordinating conjunctions discussed earlier, can help join clauses together to show interesting relationships and to provide smooth transitions.

Keeping track of each clause in your sentences will help you become a wiz at punctuation. You'll understand which clauses can stand alone (the independent clauses) and which clauses can't (the dependent clauses) and which punctuation marks are needed in your sentences. Take the time to understand and treasure the independent and dependent clauses in your writing. Each type of clause will add to your writing and help you build a rich sequence of ideas that will delight readers. Now that's something you can sink your claws into.

20

SUBJECT–VERB AGREEMENT AND SPATS

I t's a popular myth that cats and dogs don't get along. But it's not true. There are many internet videos of adorable kittens snuggled next to a big dog. And lots of people with both cats and dogs can attest to their friendship and playfulness together or at least their mutual respect. What's really going on is that *some* cats and *some* dogs don't get along, which often ends with the dog getting scratched on the nose or the cat climbing up a tree.

For subjects and verbs, it's the same deal. Subjects and verbs, when paired well, are a dynamic duo. They work together to form a remarkable invention called a sentence. However, *some* subjects do not get along with *some* verbs. They can have a spat, and that's when readers can get confused by the meaning. So, it's important to pair subjects and verbs thoughtfully to make sure they agree. This seems simple enough. For each subject (noun or pronoun), you choose a verb that agrees in number (singular or plural) with the subject, and that's that. Easy peasy, right? Not so fast. What happens if the subject of the sentence is not obvious? Or the subject is far away from its verb, obscured by various intervening phrases and asides? What if the number of the subject is unclear or downright squirrelly to determine? Don't fret. Help is on the way. First, let's review some basic rules for good subject–verb agreement.

RULES OF THUMB FOR SUBJECT-VERB AGREEMENT

Subjects (nouns and pronouns) can be singular or plural. Singular refers to one thing or one person. Plural refers to more than one thing or person. The number of the subject (singular or plural) indicates the form of the verb to use (either singular or plural). Always look to the number of the *subject* to guide you on which verb form to use.

1. Singular subjects take singular verbs. Plural subjects take plural verbs.

Her <u>handwriting</u> <u>is</u> cranky and illegible.
The <u>farm</u> <u>has</u> goats, donkeys, and an occasional marmot.
The <u>rumblings</u> <u>were</u> coming from the basement.

2. Two singular subjects joined by *and* take a plural verb.

My <u>cat</u> and <u>dog</u> <u>are</u> attending the parade.
<u>Ketchup</u> and <u>tartar sauce</u> <u>are</u> his favorite ingredients.
<u>Imagination</u> and <u>curiosity</u> <u>are</u> helpful for writing.

Exception: If a compound subject acts as a single entity or person, then use a singular verb.

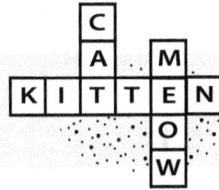

Speaker and crossword puzzle expert Ella Milford was late for her talk.

3 **A singular subject that is separated from its verb by phrases other than *and* takes a singular verb.** These phrases include *in addition to, including, as well as, along with, accompanied by, together with, besides, not, rather than,* etc.

My cat, as well as my two guinea pigs, likes cheese puffs.

Tommy, along with his cousins, is building a raft from a pickle barrel.

Polite honking rather than yelling is preferred in this instance.

TIP: Think of these intervening phrases *in addition to, along with, as well as, besides, not, rather than,* etc. and their accompanying words as asides that are not the subject of the sentence. Rather, the main subject is the star of the sentence, and thus the verb should agree with it in number.

TIP: If the sentence sounds awkward, you can change the intervening phase to another word (for instance, change *as well as* to *and*) and use a plural verb, if required. However, note that the resulting compound subject will then be the focus of the sentence.

My cat and my two guinea pigs like cheese puffs.

4 **Ignore prepositional phrases (starting with *of, after, in,* etc.) that come between a subject and a verb.**

Follow the number of the *subject*, not the object of the preposition that comes after the subject.

> The <u>aroma</u> of vanilla and chocolate brownies <u>is</u> delectable.
>
> Her large <u>assortment</u> of vaguely similar lawn ornaments <u>was</u> puzzling.
>
> Our <u>discussion</u> about the possibility of raising emus <u>was</u> getting off track.

5 **For two or more subjects joined by *or*, use the verb form that agrees with the number of the subject *closest* to the verb.**

> Dumb luck or fancy <u>lures</u> <u>help</u> him catch all the fish.
>
> Fancy lures or dumb <u>luck</u> <u>helps</u> him catch all the fish.

The same rule above applies to the pairs "either...or" and "neither... nor." Use a singular or plural verb depending on which subject is closest to the verb.

> Either a new raincoat or <u>boots</u> <u>make</u> her happy.
>
> Neither boots nor a new <u>raincoat</u> <u>makes</u> her happy.

6 **The following subjects take singular verbs because they refer to one thing or one person.** "The number of" is in this list because it refers to *one* number of things or people.

anybody	each one	everybody	nobody	somebody
anyone	either	everyone	no one	someone
each	every	neither	one	the number of

Nobody likes to take out the trash.

Anyone who sees that giant butter sculpture is going to be amazed.

Everyone is invited to the pawpaw festival tomorrow.

Each table was decorated with balloons and wizard wands.

TIP: Many of these words end with "one" or "body." This is a clue that the subject points to one person or one thing and thus uses a singular verb.

Notice that the phrase "the number of" takes a singular verb, whereas "a number of" takes a plural verb (see more details below).

The number of wrong turns I took to get here is staggering.

The number of ducks in that lake is more than I can count.

TIP: Think of "the number of" as equivalent to saying "it"— which is one number you can count, estimate, or point to, so it takes a singular verb. Variants of "the number of" such as "the actual number of" or "the total number of" also take a singular verb.

7 **The following subjects use a plural verb because they refer to more than one thing or person.**

a number of	both	few	many	several

Many salamanders have orange spots.

Few people know about the cave's secret entrance.

Both my socks have holes in them.

A number of telltale signs suggest a skunk was here.

TIP: One way to remember that "a number of" takes a plural verb is to see if it can be replaced by the word "many" or "several" in your sentence. If so, it takes a plural verb because it refers to more than one thing or person. Note that variants of "a number of" such as "a gigantic number of," "a surprising number of," or "a pitiful number of" also take a plural verb.

8 Some subjects can take either a singular or plural verb, depending on the context. Look at the number of the *object of the preposition* that follows these words to determine whether to use a singular or plural verb. If the object of the preposition is a single thing, then use a singular verb. If the object of the preposition refers to more than one thing or person, then use a plural verb.

all	any	a lot of	lots of	none
most	some	half (or other fraction or percentage)		

Most of the items in his backpack are edible.

Some of the pie is missing.

None of these saddles fit this horse.

None of the applause was for them.

All of the students are waiting for the bus.

Half of the questions were about the upcoming Sidewalk Egg Frying contest.

TIP: See if you can substitute *most, all, any, none,* and *some* with the word "they." If so, use a plural verb. If not, use a singular verb.

9. **Collective nouns refer to a group. They use a singular or plural verb depending on the context.** Use a singular verb if the collective noun refers to the group acting as a single unit. Use a plural verb if the collective noun refers to members of a group acting individually. Below are common collective nouns.

audience	couple	family	pair
class	council	flock	range
chorus	crowd	group	series
colony	dozen	herd	staff
community	faculty	majority	team

The senior <u>class</u> <u>is</u> presenting a new musical.
(The class is acting as one group or unit.)

A <u>group</u> of <u>kittens</u> <u>are</u> licking milk from their saucers.
(The kittens are acting individually.)

TIP: Collective nouns that take a singular verb are often preceded by the word "the."

TIP: Collective nouns that take a plural verb are often preceded by the word "a."

Special cases: subjects that are objects with two parts (for instance, glasses, scissors, pants, trousers) use a plural verb. However, if they are considered as a pair, they use a singular verb.

These <u>scissors</u> <u>are</u> dull.

My <u>glasses</u> <u>are</u> broken.

That <u>pair</u> of pants <u>does</u> not fit me.

My only <u>pair</u> of glasses <u>is</u> missing.

10 **When a subject and its subject complement disagree in number, the verb takes the number of the subject.** Note that *subject complements* are alternate names that complement a subject by more fully describing it. They usually appear after a "to be" linking verb such as *is, am,* and *are.*

The <u>basis</u> of our inquiry <u>is</u> the kittens and their lost mittens.

The <u>kittens</u> and their lost <u>mittens</u> <u>are</u> the basis of our inquiry.

Exception: If two subjects joined by "and" act as a single entity or idea, then use a singular verb.

<u>Research and development</u> <u>has</u> spurred many innovations.

<u>Fish and chips</u> <u>is</u> on the menu today.

11 **Some common terms and scientific and mathematical words are usually treated as singular subjects when they refer to a body of knowledge or medical term.**

aesthetics	mathematics	kinetics	semantics
economics	measles	physics	news

12 **The following Greek or Latin words are plural and usually take a plural verb.** Their singular forms are shown in parentheses below.

SUBJECT-VERB AGREEMENT AND SPATS

bacteria (bacterium)	curricula (curriculum)	minima (minimum)
crises (crisis)	data (datum)	nuclei (nucleus)
criteria (criterion)	media (medium)	strata (stratum)

QUICK GUIDE FOR SUBJECT-VERB AGREEMENT

USE A SINGULAR VERB	USE A PLURAL VERB
anybody, anyone, each, each one, either, every, everybody, everyone, neither, nobody, no one, one, somebody, someone, the number of	*both, few, many, several, a number of*
Collective noun acting as one group or unit	Collective noun acting individually
A singular subject or a compound subject that acts as a single entity or person (ignore any intervening phrases and asides)	Two singular subjects joined by "and."
Common scientific and mathematical terms (for example, *kinetics, physics, news*, referring to a body of knowledge)	Plural form of various Greek or Latin words (for example, *data, criteria, phenomena*)

SINGULAR OR PLURAL DEPENDING ON THE CONTEXT

all, a lot of, any, lots of, most, none, some; fraction (half, one-third, etc.) and percentages

Two singular subjects joined by "or" (refer to the number of the subject closest to the verb to decide the verb form to use).

A subject and its subject complement that disagree in number (the verb takes the number of the subject)

BECOMING A GOOD SUBJECT–VERB REFEREE

Now that you've learned some basic rules for subject–verb agreement, let's see if we can put them into action so your sentences will always get along nicely. Creating sentences with good subject–verb agreement is like being a good referee. As a referee, you identify the main players (subjects and verbs) in the game and make sure they play by the rules for a winning sentence. Here's how to do it.

First, correctly identify the *subject* in a sentence. Remember that the subject (noun or pronoun) likes to be the Top Dog or the main focus in a sentence, whereas the verb is like a cat in motion (or a cat sleeping or just "being"). Your first job is to spot the subject in the sentence, which isn't always easy or straightforward. The subject may not necessarily appear at the beginning of a sentence. It may appear after the verb. It may be a noun or pronoun, a single word, or a group of words. See if you can tag the subject in the following sentences.

There are many reasons why we have not cleaned out the garage. (The main subject is *reasons*.)

Swinging from a tree is fun.
(The subject is *Swinging*, a gerund.)

Somewhere among the stacks of papers on the teacher's desk
is his report on the "History of Badminton."
(The subject is *report*.)

Notice that the last example above is a bit tricky because the subject appears *after* the verb in an inverted fashion. Prepositional phrases or other words make things even stickier. If identifying the subject is challenging, try recasting the sentence in your mind to put the subject at the beginning of the sentence. In doing so, the subject is usually clear (although the sentence itself may sound awkward).

Many <u>reasons</u> <u>are</u> there why we have not cleaned the garage.

His <u>report</u> on the "History of Badminton" <u>is</u> somewhere among the stacks of papers on the teacher's desk.

Second, determine the number of the *subject* (singular or plural). After you've correctly identified the subject, then determine the *number* of the subject, that is, whether it's singular or plural. Ask yourself: does it refer to one thing or one person? Or more than one thing or person? Watch for irregular plural forms of nouns in particular (refer to Chapter 3: Naming Nouns for some examples). Also, you may have to look at the context and surrounding words to determine the number of the subject (for example, if the subject is *all, any, most, some*, and *none*, or a collective noun, the context determines the number of the subject).

Lastly, follow the number of the *subject* (singular or plural) to select the correct verb form. Once you've identified the subject and its number, here's where your refereeing skills really come into play. Follow the Top Dog subject to its associated (cat-in-waiting) verb to make sure they agree. Because of various intervening words, you may have to take a meandering path from the subject to its associated verb. Check out the following example:

subject   verb   **SINGULAR**

A <u>can</u> of cat food <u>sits</u> on the shelf.

S = Singular
P= Plural

Notice the above sentence clearly takes a singular verb. For every sentence you write, make the call on whether the verb should be singular or plural, based on the number of the *subject*. If the subject is singular, use a singular verb. If the subject is plural, use a plural verb. If the verb form does not agree in number with the subject, call Foul! Replace the verb with its correct form. Then, once you have proper subject–verb agreement…Goal!

Let's look at another example shown below. The subject is *none*. This is one of those tricky subjects in which you have to look at what comes after it to determine the number of subject. The word *onlookers* after *none* is plural, so use the plural verb form (know).

subject   **PLURAL**   verb

<u>None</u> of the curious onlookers <u>know</u> how the wedding cake fell over.

Below are a couple more examples. See if you can track the pathway from the subject to the verb form. Check them carefully to see if they agree.

Skipping as well as giggling was the main reason we were asked to leave.

His large collection of kazoos and pennywhistles, including some Irish ones, is impressive.

↪ **TIP**: Be on the lookout for multiple prepositional phases, additional words, and asides between the subject and verb. Don't let these words distract you from the correct form of the verb to use.

↪ **TIP**: Always look to the number of the *subject* to guide you on which verb form to use.

↪ **TIP**: Make sure the subject agrees in number with its associated verb, rather than nearby additional verbs.

SUBJECTS AND VERBS SHOULD AGREE, CONCUR, AND ACQUIESCE

Subject–verb disagreement is one of the most common grammar mistakes. These word squabbles are sometimes challenging to notice and fix. Intervening words between the subject and verb are frequently the culprits. Confusion over the number of the subject can also put writers in a pickle.

For these reasons, it's best to learn the basic subject–verb agreement rules well so you're confident about how to play the subject–verb game. What's more, take the time to put on your referee hat and check your writing for subject–verb agreement during editing and proofreading of your work. With time, you'll get faster at checking each sentence as you go along, even as you write. In the end, when your subjects and verbs agree and concur, your writing will purr with harmony and clarity. Then everything clicks, and all is well in your little corner of the world.

21

DANGLING AND MISPLACED MODIFIERS
(DON'T DANGLE THESE IN FRONT OF A CAT!)

Cats have a special eye for dangling things, whether it's a piece of string, shoelaces, or curtain cords. Cats can't stand it when things dangle. They must pounce and swat them down.

In grammar, words and phrases can dangle too. *Dangling modifiers* are words or phrases that mistakenly modify or describe the wrong word in a sentence. This creates confusing sentences and even unintended humor. For example, see if you can spot what's "dangling" in the following sentence:

Walking into the bookstore, my eye caught my favorite book.

Clearly, "my eye" cannot walk, even though it follows the phrase "walking into a bookstore." This phrase is a dangling modifier. It dangles around illogically in the sentence, modifying the wrong subject (in this case, "my eye"). Dangling modifiers like this one attract notice and perhaps a few giggles. Let's rewrite the sentence so it's clear who did the walking.

> As I walked into the bookstore, my eye caught my favorite book.

Some dangling modifiers can be uproariously funny and make the writer appear unaware of a silly mistake. For example,

> After rotting in the cellar for weeks, my brother Rancer brought up a basket of onions.

Lest you want your reader to think you have a rotten brother in the cellar, you may want to fix this with the following sentence:

> My brother Rancer brought up from the cellar a basket of onions that had been rotting for weeks.

DANGLING PARTICIPLES AND PHRASES

A common type of dangling modifier is called a *dangling participle*. What is a participle? Participles help complete a verb or modify a noun (act as adjectives) (see Chapter 4 for more information). They commonly end in -ing (present form) or -ed (past form). Here are some examples of participles (underlined below) that modify a noun.

The <u>napping</u> kitten

Let <u>sleeping</u> dogs lie.

Jack's <u>marinated</u> steak

Participles can also appear as phrases that modify the subject that follows them.

<u>Hissing and howling</u>, the cat threw a fit at the vacuum cleaner.

Here, "hissing and howling" is a participle phrase that describes "the cat." A *dangling participle* is a participle phrase that is not clearly connected to the word it is intended to modify. This happens when the word that follows the participle phrase is different than the word it is supposed to modify. For example,

<u>Standing on the street corner</u>, two black cats walked past me and my mother.

In the above sentence, "standing on the corner" is a participle phrase. However, it is a dangling participle because it appears to modify "two black cats," but that doesn't make logical sense, and it isn't what the writer intended. A better way to say this is as follows:

Standing on the street corner, my mother and I watched two black cats walk past us.

Putting it this way avoids the absurdity of two black cats standing on the street corner while also walking by you and your mother!

It's important to look at the subject that follows a participle phrase to see if it actually describes the correct word. If an unintended word is there, something is dangling, and you'll have to rearrange the sentence so it clearly describes what is going on. Let's review some other examples and how to fix them:

Dangling: <u>Eating pizza on the patio with Ryan</u>, three skunks appeared behind Don's shed.

Fix: Ryan and Don were eating pizza on the patio when three skunks appeared behind Don's shed.

Dangling: <u>Having finished my dinner</u>, our cat Oswald fell asleep on the dining room table. (The nerve of that cat *eating my dinner!*)

Fix: <u>After I finished my dinner</u>, our cat Oswald fell asleep on the dining room table.

You'll notice that the above fixes involve rearranging the sentence and adding a subject so it's clear who did what.

Dangling participles often appear at the beginning of a sentence. However, they can also appear at the end of a sentence.

Dangling: PJ found his wallet walking down the street. (You should be able to clear up this "walking wallet matter" right away.)

Fix: PJ found his wallet while he was walking down the street.

Other types of phrases can dangle in a sentence so they refer to the wrong thing. These types of sentences can be confusing or sound ridiculous to readers.

Dangling: Angrily, the car sped away.

Fix: He sped away angrily in his car.

Dangling: After she scratched the visitor, Laura scolded her new cat.

Fix: Laura scolded her new cat after the cat scratched the visitor.

Dangling: Cute and fuzzy, we love cats.

Fix: We love cats because they are cute and fuzzy.

Dangling: Short on change, the parking meter annoyed us.

Fix: Because we were short on change, the parking meter annoyed us.

Notice that in each example the introductory phrase does not modify the word that comes after it. These sentences needed to be rewritten so the correct word is modified.

MISPLACED MODIFIERS

Sometimes words can appear in the wrong place in a sentence so that they don't correctly describe what the writer intended. These are called *misplaced modifiers*. Some examples:

Misplaced modifier: We saw a dog run to our neighbor with three legs.

Fix: We saw a dog with three legs run to our neighbor.

Fix: We saw a three-legged dog run to our neighbor.

Misplaced modifier: The teacher spoke to the fifth grader with a gruff voice.

Fix: With a gruff voice, the teacher spoke to the fifth grader.

Fix: The teacher spoke gruffly to the fifth grader.

Misplaced modifiers also can involve adverbs, such as *only, almost, just, even, hopefully*, and *hardly*, that appear in different places in a sentence. If they appear in a different spot than what the writer intended, it can change the meaning. For example,

The cat <u>only</u> caught one fish. (implies the cat caught rather than watched or ate the fish)

<u>Only</u> the cat caught one fish. (implies just the cat, as opposed to, say, the dog, caught the fish)

The cat caught <u>only</u> one fish. (indicates the cat caught one fish and no more)

Misplaced modifiers are easier to fix than dangling modifiers are. To fix misplaced modifiers, it's necessary to move the misplaced word to the correct place in the sentence. In contrast, to fix dangling phrases, it's usually necessary to rearrange the sentence or add additional words.

ABSOLUTE PHRASES ARE NOT DANGLING MODIFIERS

Certain phrases, called absolute phrases, modify the whole sentence rather than a particular word. These phrases often begin with *considering, given, judging, provided,* and *regarding.*

That being said, I would like a refund.

Judging from her expression, the play was not going well.

Given the sorry state of affairs, we will adjourn the meeting.

As luck would have it, we had a friend who could speak Spanish.

Absolute phrases are not essential to the sentence and can be moved around without changing the meaning. They are usually set off by commas. Absolute phrases are not dangling modifiers, so they don't need to be fixed.

HOW TO SPOT AND FIX DANGLING AND MISPLACED MODIFIERS

Dangling and misplaced modifiers can confuse readers or, worse, embarrass the writer. So, it's important to be alert for dangling and misplaced modifiers in your work. Be on the lookout for them, like a cat noticing items around them that dangle or are out of place. Pounce on any phrases that are dangling and fix any words that are misplaced in a sentence. Here are a few tips.

🐾 **Look for introductory phrases that might dangle.** Participle phrases (phrases that contain -ing) are the most common type of dangling modifier. See if the introductory phrase can be moved around in the sentence, and the sentence still makes sense. If so, the phrase is probably not a dangling modifier.

🐾 **Check carefully that the subject that follows** these introductory phrases is actually the word that is being described. If not, rearrange the sentence, adding additional words if needed, so it makes sense.

🐾 **Look for phrases in the middle of a sentence** that might be misplaced and give the wrong meaning. Move the phrases closer to the word they are intended to modify.

🐾 **Make sure adverbs and qualifiers** such as *only, almost, just, even, hopefully*, and *hardly* are in the correct place in the sentence (next to or near the word they are modifying) so the meaning is clear.

Let's look at an example of how to check for and correct a dangling modifier. In the sentence below, "Racing to the airport" is a participle phrase. Participle phrases modify nouns and pronouns. Check to see if "Racing to the airport" correctly describes the words that come after it ("her briefcase")? Or is something amiss?

DANGLER

Racing to the airport, her briefcase fell on the ground.

Clearly, this sentence is illogical because it sounds like the briefcase is racing to the airport. We must rearrange the sentence and add a subject ("she") so the sentence makes sense.

Fix: Racing to the airport, she dropped her briefcase on the ground.

Or: While she was racing to the airport, she dropped her briefcase on the ground.

BEWARE DANG DANGLERS AND MESSY MODIFIERS

Dangling and misplaced modifiers are unintended word hazards. They can confuse readers or make them laugh at what you've written, depending on how illogical and ridiculous the sentence is. If you hurry through your writing and don't check that it makes logical sense, you risk flopping because of dangling and misplaced words.

Save yourself the embarrassment. Check your work carefully to make sure a dangler or misplaced word or phrase hasn't crept into your sentences unintentionally. Pounce on any that you find and reconstruct your sentences so the meaning is clear.

Wherever grammar confusion and frustration persist...

CAT GRAMMAR TO THE RESCUE!

DUELING PUNCTUATION

Should I use a comma or semicolon here?

DANGLERS

Oh, that dang dangler!

RUN-ON SENTENCES

Well, that isn't pretty!

CONFUSED WORDS

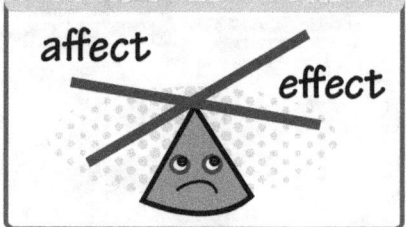

affect

effect

Which word is it?!

22

SPELLING CAT-NUNDRUMS

Supercatty-fragilistic-expialleycat-docious

ats are excellent spellers. They don't get stumped by tricky words such as *aerial, leisure, maneuver,* and *delicious*—these are already in a cat's wheelhouse. They can effortlessly train for the Cat Spelling Bee by sitting on large stacks of books and open dictionaries. They like the giant, old dictionaries the best because they have the most intriguing smells. Their favorite type of spelling bee is the round-robin. Here are some of their prize-winning spelling bee words:

GOURMET

Say: gor-MAY

Definition: someone who knows a lot about food and drink; food that is fancy or tasty

Used in a sentence: Gourmet food is the type of food you should be feeding me. What's with the bargain bin dry kibble?

FAUX PAS

Say: foe-PAW

Definition: a social blunder or gaffe; a false step

Used in a sentence: You may think it's a *faux pas* to jump on a visitor's lap, but I'm just a cat being friendly.

GEOMETRICAL

Say: JEE-o-ME-trik-al

Definition: relating to the shapes, positions, and relationships of objects

Used in a sentence: Cats know geometrical things, such as how to jump from the fireplace mantle to the coffee table in one leap.

Maybe you don't care about winning the Cat Spelling Bee. However, being a good speller has many benefits. For one thing, good spelling makes a good first impression on readers. It's like being a snappy dresser. You shine and people take notice. Precision with spelling signals a care with words, so good spelling makes you more trustworthy and credible. Poor spelling is distracting and fishy—a tipoff in scam emails and fraudulent websites. Lastly, practicing good spelling helps you learn many new words as you build your vocabulary.

WINNING TRAITS FOR GOOD SPELLING

If your spelling is not up to scratch, you can take lessons from a cat on how to improve. Cats have some excellent traits that are helpful to learn to spell well. Let's see what this "entails."

Good spelling takes precision. If you want to spell well, you have to get the arrangement of letters in words exactly right. Almost right doesn't cut it. Cats know that the placement of letters must be accurate, just as they know the placement of their cat feet on a ledge must be precise. Otherwise, they might end up dangling from the edge with only their claws. Quite a sight. Good spelling means developing a sharp eye for trouble spots. This means taking care to spell unfamiliar words, names, places, and other proper nouns correctly and consistently so readers aren't confused or put off by typos.

Perhaps you think autocorrect or spell checking software will rescue you. While these tools can be helpful, if you rely on them too much they can give you the wrong word (sometimes humorously so) or fail to flag faulty words in your writing. This sloppiness could spell disaster on a resumé or important writing assignment.

I caught a moose.

moose?

mouse!

Autocorrect thinks I am quite a hunter!

Good spelling takes a good memory. Cats learn quickly and have excellent memories for things they have learned—such as hunting skills and the sound of a can opener. To become a skilled speller, it helps to practice spelling and commit many words to memory so you're a more capable writer. Look up words you don't know in the dictionary instead of continuing to misspell them. Develop tricks for remembering how to spell words accurately. Practice. It also helps to develop a good eye for words that seem questionable and correct them if needed.

Good spelling requires persistence. Let's face it. Learning to spell well can be quite a conundrum (aka cat-nundrum) because English has so many borrowed words and roots from other languages. In fact, English can be a sloppy mess, from its odd vowel sounds, to silent letters, to various spelling irregularities. To be a good speller, you have to embrace the inconsistencies of the language. This is where the cat traits of persistence and adaptability can pay off. Cats don't give up when they encounter a confusing or odd situation. They are curious and determined, which helps them troubleshoot problems. Take it from cats and persist in learning good spelling so your writing is clear, and you don't have to waste time fixing errors.

INTRODUCING MISS PELL

Anyone who wants to become a good speller could use a helpful teacher like Miss Pell. Notice how she spells her name. It's a lot like misspell. (The thing she doesn't want you to do.) She'll be on hand as your spelling guide and memory coach in this chapter. Miss Pell conducts spelling bees, helps identify "troublesome spots" in words that make them hard to spell correctly, and can teach you about mnemonics of all kinds. Using mnemonics, she'll help you correctly spell English words for the rest of your life.

What are *mnemonics*? Where does such a goofy word come from? And how do you even pronounce this word? The word mnemonics comes from the name of the Greek Goddess of Memory. Her name was Mnemosyne. A mnemonic (pronounced ni-MON-ik) is any tool that helps you remember things. Interestingly, the word also sounds a bit like "knee-MON-ik," so when you say it, slap your knee once to help you remember that it's a useful tool. When you say Mnemosyne (pronounced ni-MOZ-o-nee) slap your knee twice. People slap their knees when they hear or see something funny or clever. In this case, your "real knee slapper" itself becomes a mnemonic—something that helps you remember something else.

Mnemonics are handy to remember many useful things. A good example is using an *acrostic*. An acrostic helps you remember the correct spelling of a word by using the initial letter in each word of a saying, such as how to spell the word *arithmetic* (A Rat In Tom's House Might Eat Tom's Ice Cream) or *geography* (George's Elderly Old Grandmother Rode A Pig Home Yesterday).

Miss Pell uses mnemonics to remember how to spell words correctly, and she'll show you how to use them to great effect. She wants you to become an expert speller. She knows that people who spell words accurately are more respected and honored than those who don't. When you seldom misspell a word you've written, readers will see you as an accurate and careful person. If you know someone over 10 years old who constantly misspells words, they are unlikely to change this bad habit. Most often they spell a word the way they think it sounds or the way they think they saw it written by someone else, so they keep misspelling it.

In this section, you'll learn how to slowly rid yourself of misspellings that can harm you for a lifetime unless you fix your memory and begin to spell words correctly. Here's how Miss Pell suggests you do it.

1   **Get the spelling of the word right first.** You must see it spelled flawlessly. It also helps to look up how to pronounce the word correctly. Some online dictionaries, such as *Merriam-Webster,* provide the audio pronunciation of words.

2   **Look for the troublesome part(s) of the word** where you could easily make a mistake in spelling it correctly (for example, the word has silent letters, tricky combinations of single or double consonants, etc.)

3   **Create a mnemonic that helps you remember the precise way the word is spelled.** Word pictures and sounds work well as mnemonics.

4   **Practice spelling and using the word correctly** so the mnemonic you created builds a new memory.

Let's see a few examples of mnemonics at work. Suppose you're having trouble spelling certain words correctly. For instance, you often misspell the word *piece* (which, by the way, doesn't give you any peace of mind). Here, Miss Pell can help. She likes to scratch below the surface of things to see what's going on. Where is the spelling trouble spot in the following word?

piece

Upon close inspection, the letters *i* and *e* appear to be the problem, as this letter combo can easily get switched around to *e* and *i*. Miss Pell suggests creating a mnemonic to visualize the correct *i-e* letter order in the word. Notice the word *piece* contains the word *pie*. When you hear the word *piece*, picture a *piece of pie*. Now you won't forget how to spell the word *piece*. By the way, Miss Pell's favorite kind of pie is shoofly pie.

PIECE

Trouble spot: p<u>ie</u>ce
Mnemonic: I had a piece of <u>pie</u>.

Here's another example. How about the word *tomorrow*? This seems like a simple word. It's used all the time, as in "Tomorrow I'll remember how to spell this word correctly, but today I'm still spelling it wrong."

to<u>mo</u>rrow

Miss Pell quickly spots your problem: the *m* and the two *r*'s. Words with sets of single or double consonants are tricky. Some are single-single combinations, double-double, single-double, double-single, or even double-double-double! To spell *tomorrow* correctly, Miss Pell suggests taking a trip right this minute "to Morrow, Ohio" (as pictured on the map below). And then you've got it! Tomorrow is looking brighter. Incidentally, if you want to wait, either later today or tomorrow, you'll still be going to Morrow.

TOMORROW

Trouble spot: to<u>mo</u>rrow
Mnemonic: Tomorrow, we're going to Morrow, Ohio.

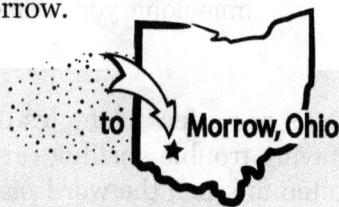

Now you can see how to use your creative noodle to permanently correct words you commonly misspell.

MISS PELL

SPELLING ADVICE

Which ending to use: -ible or -able?

Many words end in *-ible* or *-able*, and it's not always clear which ending to use. A general rule of thumb is that for words ending in -able, especially newly coined words, you can often remove the ending and still have a complete word, for example, *likeable, understandable, affordable.*

This is not true for many words that end in -ible: *compatible, credible, tangible.* If you remove the -ible ending in these words, you don't have a complete word. However, there are various exceptions, such as the words *flexible, accessible, inevitable,* and *advisable,* so the rule isn't always *dependable.*

BECOMING AN EXPERT TROUBLE SPOTTER

As Miss Pell has shown, learning to spell well requires sniffing out trouble spots in words that can trip you up. Spelling errors tend to show up in the same places and in the same patterns. If you can find the trouble spots quickly, you can more easily create a mnemonic to fix them. Here are some common types of spelling errors and solutions to fix them:

COMMON SPELLING TROUBLE SPOTS AND MNEMONIC FIXES

MIXING UP THE ORDER OF I-E OR E-I

Examples: *achieve, niece, weird, belief, fiery, perceive, siege*

Solution: The old adage of *i* before *e* except after *c* generally holds, but remember the word weird is *weird*. If necessary, create a mnemonic to remember the correct spelling.

DOUBLE OR SINGLE CONSONANTS

Examples: *broccoli, occurrence, accommodate, satellite, fulfill*

Solution: Create a mnemonic to remember the correct spelling.

MISPRONUNCIATION LEADS TO MISSPELLINGS

Examples: *arctic, lightning, miniature, raspberry, barbecue, sophomore, exhaust, courageous, espresso, ecstatic, government, privilege, temperature, probably, vegetable*

Solution: Ensure you are saying the word correctly. Create a mnemonic to remember the correct spelling.

A, E, AND I MIX-UPS

Examples: *definitely, inadvertent, apparently, unfortunately, separate, desperate, exuberance, defendant, occurrence, guidance, dependent, negligence, hindrance, preference*

Solution: Create a mnemonic to remember the correct spelling.

FOREIGN WORDS OR ROOT WORDS

Examples: *faux pas, maneuver, reservoir, bureau, connoisseur, cantaloupe, aficionado, rendezvous, bona fide*

Solution: Learn foreign roots to strengthen your spelling skills.

USE OF THE WRONG WORD

Examples: *advice/advise, affect/effect, complement/compliment, your/you're, weather/whether, accept/except*

Solution: Pay attention to the correct use of these types of sound-alike words and create a mnemonic to remember the correct one. See also Chapter 23: Commonly Confused Words.

SILENT OR MISSING LETTERS

Examples: *aisle, condemn, listen, castle, subtle, campaign, hemorrhage, mortgage, scissors, solemn, rhythm, acknowledgment, judgment, whistle, Wednesday, salmon*

Solution: Pay attention to the silent or missing letters. Create a mnemonic to remember the silent or missing letter.

-ABLE OR -IBLE ENDINGS

Examples: *accessible, acceptable, indispensable, irascible, inevitable, advisable, collectible, feasible, illegible, flexible, accountable, suggestible, fashionable, responsible*

Solution: Create a mnemonic to remember the correct spelling. See also Miss Pell's Spelling Advice box on p 191.

S AND C MIX-UPS

Examples: *license, absence, reminisce, defense, offense, presence, escape, rescue, biscuit, sauce, adolescent, ascend, oscillate, muscular, hibiscus, crescent, obscure, eschew*

Solution: Create a mnemonic to remember the correct spelling.

MNEMONIC SOLUTIONS FOR MISSPELLINGS

Creating mnemonics to remember things is fun and will help you correct misspellings permanently. As Miss Pell emphasizes, the key to creating a good spelling mnemonic is to focus on finding the spelling trouble spot(s) in the word and conjuring up a picture word or phrase that helps you remember how to spell the word. The mnemonic tool could be something personal only to you or perhaps an "inside joke"—any vivid picture or phrase that assists you.

Below are some examples of mnemonic fixes for commonly misspelled words. See if these help you remember how to spell them. Create new fixes for words you commonly misspell. Remember to be playful and persistent as you work on your spelling.

COMMONLY MISSPELLED WORDS AND MNEMONIC FIXES

ABSENCE

Trouble spot: absence

His *abs* were sore: *hence*, it explained his *absence*.

COLLEGE

Trouble spot: college

Having two L's in *college* gives you a *leg* up on life.

BROCCOLI

Trouble spot: bro<u>cc</u>oli

I cooked two cups (two c's) of broccoli in *l*iquid.

COMMITTEE

Trouble spot: co<u>mmittee</u>

The committee had two of everything (two m's, t's, and e's)

CONVENIENT

Trouble spot: conven<u>i</u>ent

The *i* in conven*i*ent is inconvenient.

DEFINITELY

Trouble spot: defin<u>it</u>ely

*Definite*ly is *finite*.

DILEMMA

Trouble spot: dil<u>emm</u>a

Our dil*emma* is finding Emma.

EXHAUST

Trouble spot: ex<u>h</u>aust

The ex*h*aust is hot.

FAMILIAR

Trouble spot: fam<u>ili</u>ar

My family is fam*iliar* with that liar.

FORTY

Trouble spot: <u>fort</u>y **40**

The 40 forts were reinforced.

GUARANTEE

Trouble spot: gua<u>ra</u>ntee

He *ra*nted about the bad gua*ra*ntee.

KNOWLEDGE

Trouble spot: knowle<u>dg</u>e

I *know* there is a *ledge*.

LICENSE

Trouble spot: li<u>ce</u>n<u>se</u>

He had *lice* and no *sense*.

NECESSARY

Trouble spot: ne<u>cess</u>ary

It was ne*cess*ary to avoid the cesspool.

NOTICEABLE

Trouble spot: notic<u>e</u>able

Notice the *e* in noticeable.

NUISANCE

Trouble spot: nuis<u>a</u>nce

My friend *Isa* is a nuisance.

OCCASION

Trouble spot: o<u>cc</u>a<u>s</u>ion

On occasion, I need two cc's of saline.

OCCURRENCE

Trouble spot: o<u>cc</u>u<u>rr</u>ence

Two c's and two r's occurred by the *fence*.

RHYTHM

Trouble spot: r<u>hyth</u>m

<u>R</u>hythm <u>H</u>elps <u>Y</u>ou <u>T</u>o <u>H</u>ear <u>M</u>usic.

SAUCE

Trouble spot: sau<u>ce</u>

The sauce is from a *can*.

SEPARATE

Trouble spot: sep<u>ara</u>te

Separate is on *par* with a *rat*.

SHERIFF

Trouble spot: she<u>riff</u>

The sheriff played a *riff* on the guitar.

SUBTLE

Trouble spot: su<u>b</u>tle

The *b* in subtle is bizarre and subtle.

WEIRD

Trouble spot: w<u>ei</u>rd

<u>We</u> are w<u>ei</u>rd.

As a final note, you'll be amazed at how well Miss Pell's mnemonic strategy works to help fix misspellings in your writing. Take the time to create a good spelling mnemonic, and it will pay off handsomely for you. You won't have to waste time again and again fixing the same spelling errors. You won't damage your credibility by having careless misspellings in your work. Good spelling will click for you, and people will recognize a new strength in your writing because it will be clear and precise. And you'll build a lifelong skill that will enhance your work and may even help you win at Cat Scrabble (a favorite cat pastime that mainly involves pawing at the letter tiles).

23

COMMONLY CONFUSED WORDS

DESSERT

DESERT

Puddles the cat is often befuddled. He commonly confuses words that sound alike but are spelled differently. Like *to, too,* and *two.* He also mixes up words that have close spellings but mean different things. Like *through, though,* and *thorough.* He uses *there* when he really means *their* and *your* when he actually means *you're.* When it rains (a good time for puddles but not for Puddles), he can't remember whether to spell it *weather* or *whether.* His only saving grace is that when he says the wrong sound-alike word aloud, no one can tell he's spelling it incorrectly. As for writing things down, Puddles is *quite* sure he should be *quiet.*

Do you get into these kinds of muddles like poor Puddles does? Mixing up words is a common challenge for many writers. English has many sound-alike and spelled-alike words that mean different things. For example, *homophones* are words that sound the same but can be spelled differently, such as see and sea. *Homographs* are words that are spelled the same but can be pronounced differently, such as bass (low note) or bass (type of fish). Then there are various words that are pronounced or spelled closely to another word, such as *lose* and *loose* or *were* and *where*.

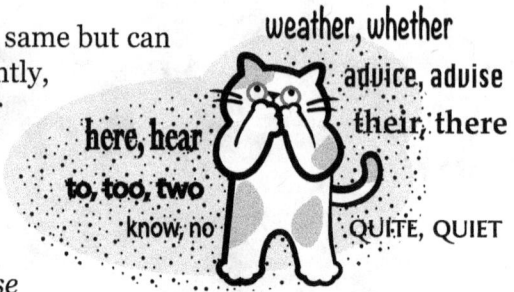

weather, whether
advice, advise
here, hear
their, there
to, too, two
know, no
QUITE, QUIET

PUDDLES THE CAT

Mixing up words, similar to spelling errors, can confuse readers and hurt your credibility as a writer. These errors can crop up anywhere in your writing, so you need to be on the lookout for them. Let's review how to recognize and fix these word mix-ups.

Learn the correct spellings of sound-alike words. Word mix-ups happen if you haven't memorized the correct spelling and definition of a given pair of sound-alike words. Is it *principal* or *principle*? *Complement* or *compliment*? If you don't get these pairs straight in your mind and continue to use the wrong word, it can reflect poorly on your writing. Here, mnemonics (first introduced by Miss Pell in Chapter 22: Spelling Cat-nundrums) can help you permanently fix in your memory the correct spellings of sound-alike words. See below for advice on creating good mnemonics and a list of mnemonic fixes for remembering commonly confused words.

Use a "smell checker" to sniff out commonly confused words. Another possible cause of word mix-ups is that you hear the sound of a word in your head, but your fingers type the wrong one. Say, *were* instead of *we're*. Or you're actually saying the word incorrectly, for example, *then* instead of *than* or *could of* instead of *could have* (or *could've*). These errors can go unnoticed in your writing until you or an alert reader catches the mistake. The important thing to notice with these word mix-ups is that their spelling usually isn't the problem. A word may be spelled correctly on its own. It is not a typo per se. It's just the wrong word in the wrong spot. This means that a spell checker program won't help. Instead, a "smell checker" is needed—to sniff out the error. That means checking that you have used the right "on the nose" word in the right place. Careful editing, proofreading, and rechecking your work can help detect and fix these types of errors.

Use the grammatically correct word. If you are grammatically confused about such things as verb tenses, that/which usage, or possessives, it's time to brush up on those areas to avoid falling into a puddle of mixed up words. Some of these types of errors are discussed in separate chapters of this book (see Chapter 4, Ready, Action, Verbs!, Chapter 18: Possessives (or Don't Touch My Paws), and Chapter 19: Independent and Dependent Clauses ("Clawses")).

USING MNEMONICS TO FIX COMMONLY CONFUSED AND SOUND-ALIKE WORDS

Below are several illustrations for often confused, sound-alike words that have totally different meanings. These are arranged for you by Miss Pell, who is not only your spelling teacher but also your memory coach. The examples below can help you remember to correctly spell sound-alike words depending on their meanings. This is done by giving you a mnemonic to vividly help you remember which word to use.

STATIONARY

Meaning: not moving
or not intended to be moved

STATIONERY

Meaning: writing paper,
especially with matching
envelopes

The first set of illustrations shows different ways of spelling *stationary/stationery*. The first drawing shows you a traffic cop with his legs apart directing traffic. His legs and belt are highlighted (like the letter A) to remind you that he must remain stationary in the middle of the street to direct traffic. If you're writing about something that does not move, such as a doghouse, a parked car, or a monument in the park, be sure to spell stationary with an A. The A is an example of a mnemonic. However, if you are thinking about stationery or materials you need to write a lEtter to your grandmother and send it to her in an Envelope, then that's a different kind of stationEry, spelled with an E.

Let's look at another example. The second set of illustrations helps you correctly spell the sound-alike words *principal/principle*. If it means the principal of your school and overall director, the word always ends with a ...*pal*. If this person disciplined you, and was not always your pal, you can remember that pretty well, too. A principal also can mean a key person who makes all the important decisions in a business or the original amount of money you put into an investment, before adding interest and profit later. These you also want to keep forever as your pal.

The word *principle* sounds exactly like *principal* but means a set of values, a philosophy, or guidelines that people use that are somewhat like a *rule* of living. They are practical or morally straight rules such as "Do unto others as you would have them do unto you." Remember the mnemonic ruLE that ends like the word principLE.

PRINCIPAL

Meaning: the head of a school, or other institution

PRINCIPLE

Meaning: a rule of action or conduct

HE**AR**

Meaning: to perceive with the ear the sound made by someone or something

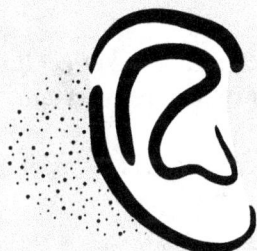

HE**RE**

Meaning: in, at, or to this place or position

here

The third set of drawings of *hear/here* are also sound-alikes. Interestingly, our English word *hear* came directly from the word *ear*. If you go to England or Australia and listen to a Cockney accent, you'll notice some people there tell you they "can't ear you." No huffy H sound at all, like an American grandfather would make when he talks without his hearing aid. The word *here* sounds exactly like hear, but it denotes a *place* or *position*, such as a friendly cat *here* on your lap. Most people mix these up only by mistake, but if you just take out your black felt tip and draw little eyeballs inside the e's in the word *here*, you should be able to find your cat. She's *here*!

Below is a list of common sound-alike words and words that are spelled or pronounced almost the same. Miss Pell has suggested mnemonic fixes for each word set to help you permanently remember the correct spelling and usage of each word.

COMMONLY CONFUSED AND SOUND-ALIKE WORDS

ACCEPT	EXCEPT
agree to, receive	exclude, leave out

Example: I'll <u>accept</u> anything <u>except</u> that.

Mnemonic: A is in the word <u>accept</u> as in Agree; E is in the word except, as in Exclude.

AFFECT

to change or make a difference

EFFECT

a result or to cause a result

Example: Christian Doppler noticed in 1842 that the <u>effect</u> on sound and light waves <u>affects</u> how we hear or see from certain distances.

Mnemonic: The A is in <u>affect</u> as in chAnge. The E is in <u>effect</u> as in rEsult.

ALL READY

prepared, completed
(adjective)

ALREADY

before or by the time
(adverb)

Example: He was <u>all</u> <u>ready</u> for the movie, but we have seen it <u>already</u>.

Mnemonic: The two L's in <u>all</u> <u>ready</u> make it complete.

ALL RIGHT

correct, acceptable, well

ALRIGHT

avoid this spelling of "all right" in formal writing

Example: She is doing <u>all</u> <u>right</u> after finding out her exam questions are <u>all</u> <u>right</u>.

Mnemonic: Two L's and two words are all right.

ALL TOGETHER

in one place

ALTOGETHER

in total, completely

Example: The cats were <u>all</u> <u>together</u>, which is <u>altogether</u> amazing.

Mnemonic: The two L's in <u>all</u> <u>together</u> are in one place.

ASSENT

support, approval, agreement

ASCENT

climb, rise

Example: The chairman gave his <u>assent</u> to her <u>ascent</u> to corporate president. The pilot made his <u>ascent</u> to 30,000 ft.

Mnemonic: The S is in <u>assent</u> as in Support. The C is in <u>ascent</u> as in Climb.

CAPITAL

seat of government, money

CAPITOL

government legislative building only

Example: In the <u>capital</u> city, you can visit the <u>Capitol</u>.
Mnemonic: The Capitol dome is in the shape of an "O."

COMPLEMENT

to enhance, make better

COMPLIMENT

to praise

Example: He <u>complemented</u> the great event with a <u>compliment</u> on her excellent work.
Mnemonic: It was k<u>i</u>nd of you to give me a compl<u>i</u>ment.

COUNCIL

Advisory or legislative group

COUNSEL

To give help or professional advice

Example: Some members of the City <u>Council</u> provided legal <u>counsel</u>.
Mnemonic: Council members use penCILs at their meetings. CounSEL = lawyers and other professionals SELL their advice.

DUAL

double, duplicate, two-fold in nature

DUEL

contest, combat, or match between parties

Example: <u>Dual</u> pistols were held by Hamilton and Burr in their notorious <u>duel</u>.

Mnemonic: Al lives in a duplex (a duAL house). E as in Engaging in a duEl.

IT'S

contraction for it is

ITS

possessive

Example: <u>It's</u> hard for a lost mitten to find <u>its</u> owner.

Mnemonic: The apostrophe in it's stands in for letters that are missing.

PAST

gone by in time; in front of or beyond

PASSED

past tense of pass

Example: It's way <u>past</u> the time for the quarterback to have <u>passed</u> the ball.

Mnemonic: PasT refers to Time. Passed is a verb that refers to movement or achievement in the past.

RIGHT

correct, not left

WRITE

act of writing

RITE

a ceremony

Example: I'll <u>write</u> about any <u>rite</u> if I feel <u>right</u> about it.

Mnemonic: Right is <u>G</u>ood. <u>W</u>rite uses <u>W</u>ords. A Ri<u>t</u>e is a Ri<u>t</u>ual.

THERE
a place

THEY'RE
a contraction of they are

THEIR
possessive of they; it belongs to them

Example: <u>There</u> in Ohio is where <u>they're</u> visiting <u>their</u> dad.

Mnemonic: The I in their indicates it belongs to several Individuals. The R in <u>there</u> indicates Right there.

TOO
excessive, also

TO
used with verbs; a preposition

TWO
number 2

Example: She wore a tutu when it was <u>too</u> hot <u>to</u> wear <u>two</u>-legged slacks.

Mnemonic: Too has an excessive number of O's.

WEATHER
<u>a</u>tmospheric conditions

WHETHER
choice between alternatives (<u>h</u>esitate or doubt)

Example: Good <u>weather</u> depends on <u>whether</u> I'm in Hawaii.

Mnemonic: Will HE? Maybe, but he Hesitates because he has lots of alternatives. The A in weather indicates Atmosphere.

YOU'RE
a contraction of you are

YOUR
possessive for you

Example: <u>You're</u> <u>your</u> own best friend.

Mnemonic: Apostrophe in <u>you're</u> stands in for missing letters.

WORDS SPELLED OR PRONOUNCED ALMOST THE SAME

ADVICE

(noun) counsel, guidance

ADVISE

(verb) to assist with suggestions and guidance

Example: The Senate not only advises colleagues to make a law, but it must also provide advice and consent.

Mnemonic: The Counselor gave her adviCe. I adviSe that you follow her Suggestions.

ASSURE

to give a commitment, to convince or relieve doubt, to affirm

ENSURE

guarantee that something will or will not happen

INSURE

contract with someone to financially protect a life or property

Example: The bank president assures all his consumers that their investments are safe. Customers ensure their bills are paid. The FDIC insures deposit holdings on all accounts up to $100,000.

Mnemonic: A in assure is usually Asked for or Affirmed. E in Ensure is guarantEE from someone trustworthy. I in insure Imposes a wrItten contact to Insure.

DESERT

a dry (sometimes sandy) area

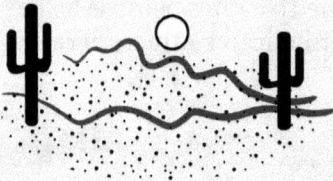

DESSERT

a tasty, after dinner treat

Example: In the Sahara Desert, you'll get no dessert.

Mnemonic: Dessert is Sweet because it has two Spoonfuls of Sugar.

DEVICE

A mechanical or mental instrument or tool (noun)

DEVISE

The act of making a useful thing (verb)

Example: Any genius can <u>devise</u> a useful <u>device</u>.

Mnemonic: A deviCe is often Clever. To deviSe Serves others.

FARTHER

A greater physical distance

FURTHER

Additional or to a greater extent (abstractly used)

Example: You must travel <u>farther</u> to <u>further</u> your education.

Mnemonic: fArther = to go a FAR distAnce. Note: This is pretty much an American and southern Canadian distinction. England and other lands of the former British Empire usually make no distinctions between these two words.

LEAD

to guide or show or surpass; also a base metal, pronounced like led

82
Pb
207.2

LED

past tense of lead

FOLLOW ME

Example: A boy named Leed could not <u>lead</u>, so his brother <u>led</u> instead. During the Civil War, the sergeant <u>led</u> his men to where they found <u>lead</u> to make ammunition.

Mnemonic: <u>Lead</u> as a verb is in the word leader. <u>Lead</u> as a metal Adds weight.

LOSE

to be defeated, to misplace

LOOSE

slack, opposite of tight

Example: A <u>loose</u> gambler will invariably <u>lose</u>.

Mnemonic: The two O's in Loose can roll around. Lose has lost one of its O's.

QUIET

very still, making little noise

QUITE

very likely, profoundly

Example: Gary was very <u>quiet</u>; he's <u>quite</u> an introvert.

Mnemonic: E before T, barely a sound; T before E, very profound.

THAN

uses a comparison

THEN

a place in time

Example: <u>Then</u> was better <u>than</u> now.

Mnemonic: Make a compArison with thAn; thEn was a timE.

WE'RE

contraction of we are

WERE

past tense of are

WHERE

a place

Example: <u>We're</u> going to <u>where</u> we <u>were</u> born.

Mnemonic: The apostrophe in <u>we're</u> stands in for letters that are missing.

PUDDLE PLAY

This chapter has shown you how to be on the lookout for commonly muddled words and how to fix them using imaginative memory tricks, also known as mnemonics. A well-trained memory can help you create thousands of mnemonics in your lifetime. There are oodles of different types of mnemonics you can use to help you remember all manner of things.

From the above examples, you can see how to use the letters in words to help you remember the different meanings of sound-alike words. But letters can help you remember names too. Suppose you are having a hard time remembering the name of your new friend Ellen. What's the solution? Miss Pell suggests you take out your imaginary felt tip pen and write her name on her forehead (in your imagination) using the letters LN (which sound like Ellen). You'll never forget her name again because each time you see Ellen, you'll see those LN letters.

And what about our friend Puddles? He has a typical fluffy, cuddly cat name you might need to fix in your memory or it could be easily forgotten. In your imagination, you might first see a large puddle. Then see the muddy brown surface begin to swirl and make waves. Suddenly, a big cat jumps out and shakes off all the water from his fur right onto you. Whew! Good thing this all happens only in your imagination, or you might get soaked. Incidentally, a few brown splotches of water stick to his fur like giant puddle markings. Now, you may have trouble getting the name Puddles out of your mind.

The best mnemonics for remembering commonly confused words are the ones you make up yourself. If they're good enough, you'll have trouble forgetting them. And that's just what you want. As for Puddles, he now uses mnemonics whenever he can to keep words straight. If he creates vivid enough images in his mind, these solutions will always "stick" with him.

Miss Pell

A centuries-old typo

Commonly confused words and multiple variant spellings of the same word go back centuries. We've had standard English spellings only in the last 300 years or so, which has contributed enormously to cultural and scientific advancements throughout the world. If you check early drafts of Shakespeare and the founding documents of the United States, you'll see instances of spelling variants or what we would call "errors" nowadays. Even the *U.S. Constitution* includes a few stray typos, inconsistencies, and variant spellings. For instance:

> From the Preamble, the British variant spelling of defense is used: "We the People...provide for the common defence..."

> Article 1, Section 10, incorrectly uses the word *it's* instead of *its*: "No State shall...lay any Imposts or Duties on Imports or Exports, except what may be absolutely necessary for executing it's Inspection Laws."

> The text also contains instances of an older spelling of the word *choose*: "The House of Representatives shall chuse their Speaker and other Officers..."

Even in important documents, texts, and speeches, word problems and inconsistencies can crop up. Our best *defense* is to *choose* to try to ensure our writing is always *its* best.

24

MEOW'S THE TIME TO LEARN A NEW WORD

juxtaposition
paradox KOWTOW
obtuse
sanguine meticulous
quasar ostentatious
VORTEX conundrum

ats are constantly on the lookout for new things: new treats, new smells, new things to jump on, new napping places, new toys, new objects that make perfectly good replacements for real toys (such as paper bags, boxes, string, dust bunnies, milk jug rings, pencils, etc.). They're always exploring and learning. This is what makes a cat's life a daily, exciting adventure.

Although cats have limited vocabularies, they learn new words every day, just for fun. For example, they might like to try out a new trill that, loosely translated, means "Why are you still in bed when the sun has been up for an hour?" Or they'll practice a new growl from their window perch that informs you, "That fat squirrel is eating the bird seed again!"

When cats learn a new word, they feel happy and pleased with themselves. New words give them a bigger bag of tricks to communicate with people around them—though we humans are sometimes too dense to understand what they're trying to say.

Learning new words can help you communicate better, too. And here's a little secret: new words are like having a new musical note or paint brush to play with. The more words you know, and have available on the tip of your tongue, the richer and more magical your writing can be. A bounty of good words gives you a larger palette to create something amazing.

The odd thing about new words, however, is that sometimes they aren't really new at all. You may have heard or seen the same ones many times. They show up like a vaguely familiar person whose name you have forgotten. These words stare at you blankly and annoyingly on the page, and even though you've looked them up in the dictionary multiple times, for the life of you, you still can't remember what they mean.

What's the solution to this conundrum (aka, sticky situation)? The trick to learning a new word is to capture it like a gemstone, look up what it means, and use a handy method to remember it permanently before it slips through your fingers again. This calls for a game!

USING "PICTURABLE EQUIVALENTS" TO REMEMBER NEW WORDS

Ever heard of this poem?

Thirty days hath September
April, June, and November.
All the rest have thirty-one
Excepting February alone,
Which is twenty-eight days clear
And twenty-nine each leap year.

This is an example of a verse mnemonic, which helps you remember how many days are in each month. Mnemonics (ni-MON-niks) are wonderful "mind tools" introduced over 5,000 years ago by ancient teachers. These teachers showed us how to remember things long before most people could write. As mentioned earlier, this word comes from the name Mnemosyne (ni-MOZ-o-nee), the Greek Goddess of Memory.

There are hundreds of useful mnemonic techniques, but you'd have to take a memory course to learn them. Once you learn different techniques, you'll discover thousands of useful mnemonics that will make you not only a great student but a person with an incredible memory.

MNEMOSYNE

Since the purpose of this book is to help you learn "cat grammar" and become a good writer, this chapter is devoted to teaching you how to remember new words, rather than to develop an excellent memory. We recommend any book by Harry Lorayne for that purpose (see References and Resources on p 237).

Every good writer seems to have a good vocabulary. The best mnemonic technique for increasing your vocabulary is to use *picturable equivalents* or pictures that illustrate the sounds of words. In the memory business, it is called a PIQUIVALENT. As you may recall, we learned about mnemonics and creating word pictures in Chapters 22 and 23—as a tool to help you become a good speller and avoid commonly confused words.

Anyone with a strong imagination can create a good piquivalent for remembering a new word, by focusing on the sound of the word (or multiple parts of the word) to "picturize" its meaning. Some people are genius at this exercise. Others seem to struggle with it. However, the more you try it, the more you'll become remarkably strong at creating useful piquivalents for new words you want to learn.

As an example, let's consider the word *paradox* (PAIR-a-doks), which means a *contradiction* or a *puzzling mismatch*. A piquivalent to illustrate this word might be a "pair of docs (doctors)." One doc is short and blonde, the other thin and brunette; in other words, they are contradictory. PAIR + DOCS = paradox. This scene helps illustrate something that is a mismatch and pairs the sound of the word with its meaning.

Here's another example. Consider the word *trenchant* (TRENCH-ant), meaning *sharp, piercing,* or *biting*. A piquivalent for this word might be a giant, biting ant carving a trench in the ground. TRENCH + ANT = trenchant. The picture of a biting ant digging a trench emphasizes something sharp or biting.

PARADOX

Say: PAIR-a-doks
Meaning: contradiction,
puzzling mismatch

A pair of doctors

TRENCHANT

Say: TRENCH-ant
Meaning: sharp, piercing,
or biting

Ant climbing out of a sharp trench

Let's try a few more. How about the word *incognito*, which means something hidden or disguised. We can break that word into several sounds, such as *in + cog + nito* (sounds like *needle*). Here we picture a cog with a needle hidden in there to illustrate something hidden or *incognito*.

What about the word *truculent*, which means aggressive or combative? Again, we can break that word into several sound parts, such as truck + u + lent. We can picture an angry guy in a truck with the words U-Lent on the side. The guy is mad because you lent him the truck, and he doesn't want to return it yet.

Below are two more examples of piquivalents for the words *loquacious* and *hyperbole*. These words are harder to "picturize" than other words. This is because it's more difficult to create sound-alikes from parts of these words. Take the word *loquacious*, meaning talkative. The main sounds in this word are "low" and "quay." Quay means a dock or wharf for loading ships. If you know what quay means, you can use that sound. If not, then you could try the (imperfect) sound "quak." Here, you could picture a small (low) chatty duck quacking at a bigger duck. *Hyperbole* is somewhat easier. You could picture a small, high-strung dog acting hyper (excitable) next to a large bowl with an E on it, which "bowls" you over.

INCOGNITO

Say: in-cog-NEET-o
Meaning: disguised, concealed

Cogs with a needle hidden in there

TRUCULENT

Say: TRUCK-u-lent
Meaning: aggressive, combative

Guy with a big truck u lent him; he is mad because he doesn't want to give it back yet

LOQUACIOUS

Say: low-KWAY-shus
Meaning: talkative, chatty

Low (or small) duck quacking and talking at a large duck

HYPERBOLE

Say: hi-PER-bowl-e
Meaning: exaggeration, overstatement

Big (hyper) bowl with large E on the bowl

Here are some tips for creating good piquivalents for new words you want to learn:

1 **Look up the word's primary meaning and how to pronounce it correctly in a dictionary** (some online dictionaries, such as *The Merriam-Webster Dictionary*, provide the audio pronunciation of words).

2 **Repeat the word aloud several times to see what pictures emerge in your mind when you say the word.** If you need to, break the word into several sound parts and see if you can create pictures for each of those parts.

3 **It's best to create pictures of concrete things** (i.e., tangible objects) rather than abstract concepts or words.

4 **Create pictures from the actual word only.** Avoid adding additional, distracting images or sounds that are not part of the word.

5 **Make the piquivalents vivid, silly, exaggerated, and memorable.** Have fun!

Now, it's your turn! Try to create piquivalents for the following words: *catalyst, dogma, Chickasaw, conundrum, effulgent, strident, cantankerous.*

There are many reference books and word websites you can consult to help you find new words to learn (see a short list of new words on p 217). Below is a sampling of words that are handy for writing. How many of these do you know? For any words that are new to you, consider creating a piquivalent to remember them. This will help expand your vocabulary and stretch your imagination, something helpful to every writer.

epiphany

winnow

quandary

churlish

sanquine

tectonic

NEW WORD LIST - HOW MANY DO YOU KNOW?

aberration	epiphany	obfuscate	tectonic
anathema	eschew	obsequious	tempestuous
auspicious	evanescent	ostentatious	unctuous
bellicose	feckless	precipitous	usurp
chicanery	ineffable	quandary	vacuous
churlish	jejune	sanguine	vehement
clandestine	lugubrious	sardonic	vitriolic
deleterious	nemesis	scurrilous	winnow
enigma	nihilism	superfluous	zephyr

In addition, the English language has been bequeathed with many delightful foreign phases and root words. Learning these can add a bit of flair and *je ne sais quoi* (a certain indescribable something) to your writing. Memorizing common foreign prefixes and suffixes can also help you learn thousands of new words. Below is a sampling. See if you can create a piquivalent to remember any foreign phrases that are new to you.

NEW FOREIGN PHRASE LIST

ad nauseam	*carte blanche*	*fait accompli*	*modus operandi*
alma mater	*caveat emptor*	*ipso facto*	*persona non grata*
avant garde	*déjà vu*	*je ne sais quois*	*prima donna*
bona fide	*en masse*	*laissez faire*	*status quo*
bon voyage	*faux pas*	*mea culpa*	*writ large*

FINDING AND USING NEW WORDS

Finding new words is easy because they're all around you: in books, grocery stores, conversations, social media, TV, crossword puzzles, speeches, signs, movies, songs, and websites. Some new words have intriguing sounds or hidden backstories—if you're the curious type and want to investigate them further.

Each new word you find is a secret world waiting to be discovered—one simple word can contain centuries of meaning and layers of nuance and emotion. Plus, some words are simply scrumptious to say! Be on the lookout for new words that are particularly juicy and enticing to you. Savor them. Consider collecting any beauties you find in a special journal or notebook for later use.

Any new word you uncover is yours to keep and use whenever you want. It can be a potential new acquaintance or perhaps a lifelong friend. You just have to introduce yourself and take the time to get to know it. Consider the word *garrulous,* meaning talkative.

Hello, garrulous! You're a fun sounding word. What do you mean?

Oh, what a great question! This affords me the opportunity to tell you all about myself. I've been told I'm chatty, which truth told I do like to talk. People say I'm long-winded, perhaps babbling, maybe even gassy, as well as verbose. Some call me digressive too. Can you believe that!

Actually, I—

If you ask me, you'd be gabby too if you rhymed with "perilous" and "querulous"! Ha! Actually, do you have a minute? Because that reminds me of a childhood story—

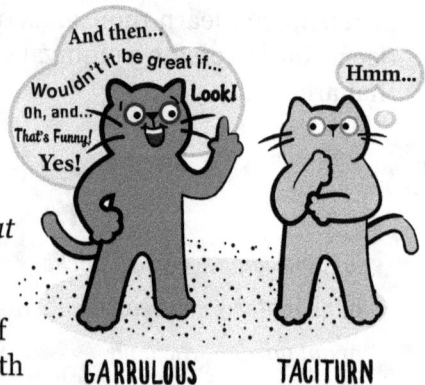

GARRULOUS   TACITURN

Garrulous will talk your ear off until you want to put it in a jar with a tight-fitting lid. Alternatively, there's *taciturn,* meaning quiet.

Hello there, taciturn! We've never met before. How's it going?

Fine.

Well, I just met garrulous. Garrulous is a kick, but a bit chatty. Have you two met?

No.

I see. Well, maybe I can introduce you sometime, and we can all be friends.

Hmm.

Using new words you've just met can be a bit awkward. It's a bit like stepping out in a shiny pair of shoes three sizes too big. You may feel self-conscious and clumsy. Maybe you're unsure how a new word is pronounced or are unclear about its subtle shades of meaning. You may use it wrong or get it mixed up with a similar sounding word. People may laugh. But that's okay, because you, as a writer or aspiring writer, have endeavored to befriend all manner of words, and eventually you'll learn to use each new word masterfully.

Start gingerly. Don't go out too far on a limb at first. Test out a new word in a casual conversation, say, with your cat first. Then maybe try it out on your good friend or little sister or brother. See how they like it. If they seem intrigued or wowed, you may have found a good word!

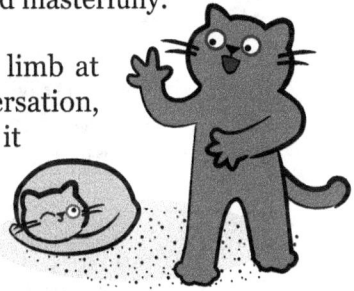

Notice that after you learn a new word, you'll see it everywhere—in books, conversation, movies, etc.—like it's been right under your nose your whole life. When this happens, listen carefully to how it's being used and what impact it has on you when you hear it. Does it stop you in your tracks? Does it make you feel like singing, or does your breath quicken when you think of it? What undercurrents of meaning and color does the word convey? You'll notice that the most powerful speeches, sermons, and soliloquies use the right word at the exactly the right moment for the greatest effect. Use these experiences as a guide to help you shape gorgeous, flowing sentences using your new words.

Finally, a word about using new words. Avoid using obscure or big words meant to stump or intimidate people. Try to match your word choices to the audience you're trying to reach. Don't bewilder them with a string of big, impressive-sounding words. Some of the simplest words are also the most profound. If one of the noblest quests of a writer is to illuminate and explain the world to others, then choose the most thoughtful, expressive words you can find—as a bridge of understanding for your readers.

Head Scratcher

BIG WORDS

What's the longest English word?

When it comes to big words, the 29-letter word *floccinaucinihilipilification* has a lot going for it. This preposterously long word, meaning "the action or habit of estimating something as worthless" according to the *New Oxford American Dictionary*, is considered one of the longest words in the English language. While the word is mainly regarded as a humorous curiosity, rather than a useful word, its origins are delightful. The word comes from the combination of four Latin words: *flocci* ("tuft or wisp"), *nauci* ("trifle"), *nihili* ("nothing"), and *pili* ("hair"). These words with similar meanings appeared together in a Latin grammar book at Eton College in the mid-1700s. Students apparently strung the peppy sounding words together and added "-fication" to the end to create this ridiculous but fun new word. Incidentally, if you use this word a lot you may be considered a *sesquipedalian*, which means a long word or a person who is long-winded or uses big words.

25

CONSISTENCY CAT-ISTHENICS

SPELLING
COMMAS
VERB TENSE
HYPHENS

Cats like consistency—until they don't. They like to eat the same foods, nap in the same place for weeks, and wake you up at the same time each morning. Then, for no apparent reason, they hate their normal food and find new, unusual sleeping spots—like on the top of the washing machine. (They still like to wake you up at the crack of dawn though!) When cats are not consistent, it can throw you off and can even be a bit confusing or frustrating (for example, they'll suddenly reject an expensive can of gourmet food).

Readers like consistency, too. They like to know what's going on and what's what when they're reading. If they encounter inconsistent spellings of names or places, shifting verb tenses, or other grammar irregularities, they may feel less certain, and less thrilled, about what they're reading.

Consistency lends a certain credibility and professionalism to writing. It gives writing a sturdiness and logical structure upon which to build an imaginative work. It signals that the writer takes care of details and respects the reader's time. In this way, consistency boosts the impact of a writer's creation because the writing is clear, and readers don't get tripped up by murky details.

This is not to say that your writing should have no surprises and should always conform to rigid rules. Quite the contrary. Writing can be daring and fanciful and still be consistent. It can be inventive, riveting, and playful, and at the same time have a sound structure and syntax. In other words, it's best to surprise readers with a clever turn of phrase or intriguing plot twist rather than with unintentional misspellings or other inconsistencies.

CONSISTENCY INSISTENCY

As a writer, you'll shine if you insist on consistency. What does consistency in writing mean exactly? Consistency is a prized principle among writers and editors. It means to follow basic grammar conventions and apply style points uniformly. That means spelling names and terms the same way and using similar verb tenses, punctuation, capitalization, and formatting throughout your work. This attention to detail gives writing a smooth, polished appearance as opposed to a ragtag look. Being consistent saves time because can you decide on a style ahead of time and stick with it throughout instead of having to make a style decision each time.

An important tool for ensuring consistency is a *style guide*. Style guides are agreed-upon style rules and conventions to follow for a specific piece of writing, publication, or organization. They include preferred spellings, comma and hyphen rules, and formatting and design standards. Style guides save time because by using them you can ensure your writing is consistent by following the guidelines.

Professional style guides used in the United States include *The Associated Press Stylebook*, *The Elements of Style*, and *The Chicago*

Manual of Style. There are many other specialized style guides used around the world, such as *MLA Handbook for Writers of Research Papers* and *Web Style Guide: Basic Design Principles for Creating Web Sites.* If you're writing for a particular publication, field, or organization, you should follow its preferred style guide. For general use or for your own writing purposes, you can create your own style sheet instead to ensure consistency (see more about style sheets in the Consistency Advice box on p 232). Note that a style guide acts as a guide, rather than a rigid set of rules—allowing you to use your best judgment as you write.

CONSISTENCY CHECKS

Let's review some of the main areas of consistency to check in your work. These include spelling, punctuation, verb tense, and tone.

Consistent spelling. Consistent spelling is a no-brainer for good writing. However, spelling irregularities can easily creep into writing and hurt your credibility. For example, suppose you're reading an adventure story, and the author mentions the character "Fredrick." However, you also notice the author uses the names "Frederik" and "Fredric." You wonder: Is this the tale of three Freds (different characters) or all the same character? These spelling discrepancies distract you and break the spell of the story.

FREDRICK   FREDERIK   FREDRIC

That's why it's important as a writer to ensure that you spell names for people, places, and things consistently and accurately. Examples include names of characters or real people (Kathryn Sullivan, Catherine Sullivan), locations (Addelane, Addle Lane), companies and organizations (the Museum of Meows, the Meow Museum), and things (disk, disc).

Catching spelling inconsistencies for proper names for people, places, and things is especially challenging because standard spell checking software doesn't flag these. The best way to prevent inconsistencies is to create a running list or "style sheet" of preferred spellings of names and terms in your work. Then, you can check them for consistency while you're writing or during the editing or proofreading process. Specialized editing software can also help you find and correct spelling inconsistencies (and other types of consistency problems).

Commas. Consistent use of commas will save you time and make your writing clearer to readers. An example is whether or not to use a series comma (aka serial or Oxford comma). A series comma is the last comma before "and" (or other conjunction) in a list of three or more items (see Chapter 14: Comma Corral (and Parentheses too) for examples). For example, the comma after "cats" in the following sentence is a series comma.

Cheetahs, caracals, jungle cats, and leopards live in Africa.

Although use of the series comma is optional, many professional style guides (such as *The Chicago Manual of Style*) recommend its use. Series commas help clarify each item in a list and prevent confusion. However, some style guides, such as *The Associated Press Stylebook*, do not use series commas. The important point here is to adhere to one comma style and use it consistently.

Hyphens. Hyphens are used to join two words or parts of words together (for example, a well-fed cat). Hyphens are useful to show readers that certain words go together and to help clarify meaning. However, in truth, hyphens can be temperamental, flighty rascals. They can appear in one instance and suddenly disappear on the following page. Unless you're careful about using them consistently, hyphens can be distracting and annoying to readers.

Whether to use hyphens in various instances is generally a matter of style and taste, although there are some general guidelines to help bring order to the hyphen hassle. Style guides can help you make decisions about when to hyphenate words. You can also use a standard dictionary such as *Merriam-Webster's* as a hyphen style guide. Here are a few hyphen guidelines and points to consider.

Prefixes. Prefixes appear at the beginning of words to form a new word. They include anti-, bio-, pre-, post-, semi-, mid-, multi-, non-, inter-, etc. In general, prefixes are not hyphenated in regular words. For example,

> semisweet chocolate
>
> multipurpose room
>
> prenatal care

However, hyphens are generally used (1) if they appear before capitalized words or numbers, (2) to separate double letters in words, (3) after the prefixes ex-, self-, cross-, and all-. Consult a dictionary for more guidance.

> mid-1990s
>
> pre-Cretaceous period
>
> anti-inflammatory
>
> ex-governor
>
> self-evident
>
> all-encompassing

Suffixes. Suffixes appear at the end of words to create a new word. Suffixes include -like, -less, -wise, -wide, and -type. Suffixes are usually not hyphenated. However, some suffixes (-fold, -odd) are hyphenated. Consult a professional style guide or a dictionary for guidance.

citywide
motionless
catlike
10-fold
Amish-style
bold-type

Compound modifiers. Compound modifiers are multiple words that act like an adjective. A hyphen is generally used between the words to signal that they act as one unit to describe a noun.

cat-friendly furniture
sweet-smelling taffy
hair-raising mystery
well-known author
low-quality fabric

If the compound modifier appears *after* rather than *before* the noun, a hyphen is generally omitted. Note, however, that some style guides use a hyphen in those instances.

The furniture is cat friendly.

The taffy is sweet smelling.

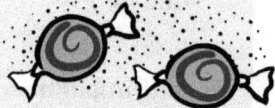

Compound words. Compound words are two words that go together as a single unit. They can be hyphenated, closed up, or two words depending on the style. Consult a dictionary for guidance.

merry-go-round
editor-in-chief
homemade
blind spot

Numbers and Fractions. Fractions and spelled out numbers between 21 and 99 are usually hyphenated. Numbers used in compound adjectives are usually hyphenated.

> one-third, five-eighths, three-fourths
> forty-three puff pastries
> ten-minute walk

Color combinations. Usually, colors are hyphenated.

> blue-green
> reddish-orange

Adverbs ending in -ly. Hyphens are not used between adverbs ending in -ly + an adjective or participle.

> highly aggravating
> unwaveringly accurate
> vaguely familiar

As you can see, hyphen use can vary a lot between style guides. Use your best judgment based on your chosen style guide and dictionary and be consistent.

Capitalization. Being consistent with capitalization means checking that the same style is used for terms, titles, and headings.

> Internet, internet
> Section 2, section 2
>
> The Missing Clue, The missing clue,
> THE MISSING CLUE

Dates. Dates can be presented in various formats, which should be consistent throughout.

March 3, March 3rd, 3/3, 3 March

Periods. Periods can be used or omitted in abbreviations for titles, places, and times. Decide on one format and stick with it.

Prof. Furbus or Prof Furbus
US or U.S.
Ph.D. or PhD
9 a.m. or 9 am

Quote marks, parentheses, and brackets. For consistency and clarity, ensure that quote marks, parentheses, and brackets occur in pairs and ending marks aren't missing.

Numbers. Presentation of numbers should be consistent rather than a mixture of spelled out numbers and numerals. Note that many style guides recommend spelling out numbers from one to nine and using numerals for numbers 10 and higher. However, other style guides spell out numbers or use numerals in all cases. Follow the style guide of your choice or create your own style sheet for presenting numbers consistently.

Maine has fifty-seven active lighthouses, whereas Virginia has only nine.

We picked 10 apples and 12 peaches.

Where did the 147 jelly beans in the jar go?

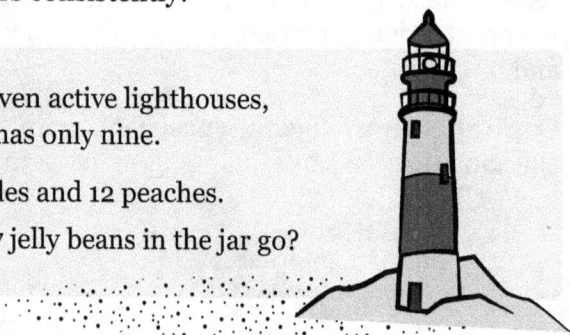

Verb tenses. Randomly switching from one verb tense to another (for example, present tense and past tense) can be unsettling to readers. It makes your writing seem chronologically fuzzy. For example, notice the shifting, jagged timeline in the following sentences.

> Harold made up his mind as he walks to the plate. He decided to be patient and is waiting for the perfect pitch. This frustrates the pitcher and caused his teammates to shuffle around the field.

Here's a new version using the present tense consistently. Notice the story unfolds more smoothly and clearly.

> Harold makes up his mind as he walks to the plate. He decides to be patient and wait for the perfect pitch. This frustrates the pitcher and causes his teammates to shuffle around the field.

For verb tense consistency, decide ahead of time which tense will work best for your particular piece of writing and use it throughout your work. For more information on verb tenses, see Chapter 4: Ready, Action, Verbs!

Parallelism. Parallelism (aka parallel construction) means using a similar grammatical structure to present words, phrases, and clauses in a sentence or group of sentences. This gives writing balance and symmetry. Let's see an example:

> Her adventures this summer included exploring a cave, riding a horse, and hiking in Utah.

Notice in the above sentence that each item in the list is grammatically similar. This structure helps improve readability and gives the sentence a pleasant rhythm. A common error is to present ideas with an inconsistent sentence structure, in which the phrases are not "parallel" or similar.

Inconsistent: Cats like to jump, napping, and looking out the window.

Consistent: Cats like jumping, napping, and looking out the window.

Inconsistent: The yellow bike has 10 speeds, the red bike has 18 speeds, and there are 21 speeds on the green bike.

Consistent: The yellow bike has 10 speeds, the red bike has 18 speeds, and the green bike has 21 speeds.

He drove the truck, whereas she chauffeured the bus.

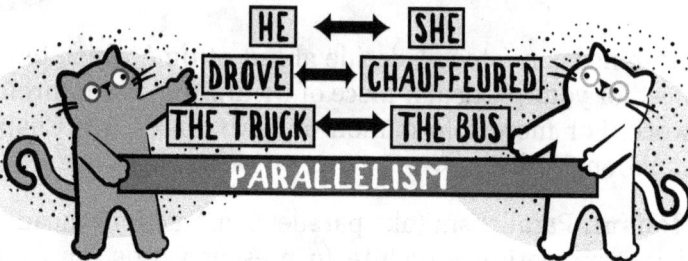

Parallel construction makes writing clearer because readers can quickly grasp the patterns and see comparisons and contrasts more easily. In addition, parallelism can give writing a powerful cadence and rhythm. Note the repetition and building momentum in the opening lines of *A Tale of Two Cities* by Charles Dickens that use a string of similar sounding clauses:

It was the best of times, it was the worst of times, it was the age of wisdom, it was the age of foolishness, it was the epoch of belief, it was the epoch of incredulity, it was the season of Light, it was the season of Darkness, it was the spring of hope, it was the winter of despair....

Tone and mood. All writing has a certain tone that conveys a specific mood, style, and attitude. It could be humorous and playful. Or angry and biting. It could be serious and academic. Or wry and witty. These are choices that a writer can make to impact tone. An informal, breezy tone prepares readers for an easygoing stroll. A ranting tone signals they may be in for a wild ride.

A consistent tone strengthens a piece of writing because readers know what to expect. They can anticipate the reading journey—a leisurely ride or a thrilling sprint. It's important to decide on the type of tone you want to use depending on your audience and purpose. Then maintain a consistent tone throughout. As you're writing, check for unexpected shifts in tone that can be jarring to readers and can muddle your message.

CONSISTENCY CHECKLIST

✔ Are spellings of names of people, places, and things consistent?

✔ Is the use of punctuation marks (commas, hyphens, periods, etc.) consistent?

✔ Is the formatting of text (fonts, font sizes, case, etc.) consistent throughout?

✔ Are the styles for capitalizations, dates, and numbers consistent?

✔ Do all quote marks, parentheses, and brackets appear in pairs (no unpaired marks)?

✔ Are verb tenses consistent throughout?

✔ Are sentences and items in bulleted or numbered lists structured consistently (using parallel construction)?

✔ Are the tone and mood of the writing steady and consistent?

CONSISTENCY ADVICE · *Miss Pell*

Create your own style sheet

A style sheet is a list of conventions and style rules to follow in your writing. These standards may include preferred spellings, punctuation, capitalization, formatting, and other style or design points. You can create your own style sheet for each piece of writing you do or use an existing style guide (such as *The Chicago Manual of Style* or *The Associated Press Stylebook*) and standard dictionary. Once you create a style sheet, you can keep a running list of style items as you go along so you can be consistent. This greatly simplifies the process of checking for consistency as you write or during the editing process.

MY STYLE SHEET

☑ **Preferred Character Name Spelling**
  Protagonist - *Fluffie*
  Antagonist - *Bigg Dog*
  Other Characters - *Blackie, Avalon*

☑ **Tone** - *Humorous, Adventurous*

☑ **Formatting Style**
  Bullet points - *Cat paws in place of bullet points*

☑ **Use Series Comma**

☑ **Verb Tense** - *Past tense*

☑ **Numbers** - *Spell out numbers one to nine; use numerals 10 and higher*

CONSISTENCY IS THE ONLY CONSTANT

Consistency is one of the great constants in writing that will bring professionalism and coherence to your work. Consistency helps smooth out any raggedy edges and brings a sense of craftsmanship to your writing as you make informed style choices. Though it takes some effort to ensure consistency in spelling, style, punctuation, verb tense, and other areas, it will pay off in terms of improved readability and a better reading experience for your audience. Now that's showing a bit of cat style.

HOLD ON TO YOUR MITTENS: WRAP-UP

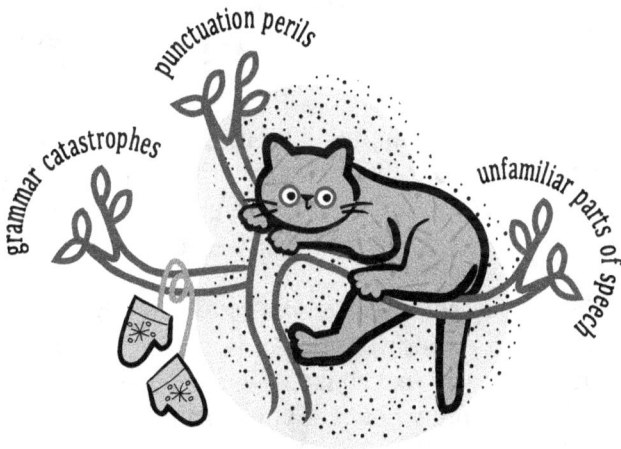

punctuation perils

grammar catastrophes

unfamiliar parts of speech

Well, it's the end of the book, and at long last you made it through your grammar journey. Congratulations! Remember back at the beginning when you were just a wee kitten and didn't always know what was what? Some grammar rules may have seemed treacherous and scary. You may have gotten stuck up a language problem tree and didn't know how to get down.

But with bright-eyed enthusiasm and determination, you navigated your way through unfamiliar parts of speech, the perils of punctuation, and common grammar catastrophes with style. Now you're a strong, confident cool cat with the grammar skills to shine in all the writing you want to do.

So, what will you do with your new grammar skills? What will you be inspired to create?

What about composing a stirring speech about your lifelong dream, such as becoming a pilot? Or penning a sci-fi mystery about far-flung planets? You could also write about a tasty new recipe or craft detailed instructions for a video on how to build a cat climber, all the while using correct grammar to communicate most effectively.

With a sturdy grammar foundation, you'll be able to express yourself more clearly with precision, creativity, and style. In addition, with your new mnemonics skills, you'll be able to easily learn new words to expand your vocabulary. And if you use a style sheet and pay attention to consistency, your writing will have a polished, professional look that people will admire. With each new creative project you undertake, you'll enhance your grammar expertise and impact on readers even further.

That's what excellent grammar skills can do for you. They will bring order and confidence to your writing, but they will also allow you the freedom to express yourself in many different ways—even allowing you to veer off the beaten path a bit to be creative in your own way.

So, don't lose the lessons you've learned in this book. Hold on to your grammar skills wherever you go. Build on them and brush up on areas where you still feel shaky. Use *Cat Grammar Guide* as an inspiring reference tool whenever you start a new writing journey. Put your best paw forward.

For even more creative encouragement, look for our next book called *Cat Writing Guide* where you can learn about writing basics, such as plot, theme, setting, and characters, and get cat-inspired advice for nurturing a creative writing life.

So, as we close the final pages on this book, we and all the Grammar Cats bid you a hearty farewell and wish you the best of luck in your creative endeavors.

Stay bright-eyed and curious about grammar and language. The world awaits your dazzling new writing creations.

REFERENCES AND RESOURCES

The following resources were helpful reference materials during the writing of *Cat Grammar Guide*.

Grammar books

Eats Shoots and Leaves: The Zero Tolerance Approach to Punctuation, by Lynne Truss, Avery, 2006.
A playful, instructive look at punctuation and how its proper use can help prevent confusion and bring clarity to writing.

Elements of Style, 4th ed., by William Strunk, Jr. and E. B. White, Pearson, 1999.
A concise, classic book on grammar and style.

Grammar Girl's Quick and Dirty Tips for Better Writing, by Mignon Fogarty, St. Martin's Griffin, 2008.
A best-selling grammar book by the award-winning author and podcaster.

Grammarly.com
A grammar, spell-checking, and writing style service; their website provides many grammar and writing resources.

Rebel With a Clause: Tales and Tips from a Roving Grammarian, by Ellen Jovin, Mariner, 2022.
An informative book based on the author's experience setting up "The Grammar Table" outside her Manhattan apartment to answer grammar questions from by passers-by. It was a sensational success! This book also includes fascinating details about the English language.

Saxon Grammar and Writing: Student Workbook Grade 5, 1st ed., by Christie Curtis, Stephen Hake, and Mary Hake, Steck-Vaughn, 2009.
Beginning workbook for students to learn and practice grammar and writing no matter their grade level.

Style guides

The Associated Press Stylebook, 55th ed., Basic Books, 2020.

The Chicago Manual of Style, 17th ed., University of Chicago Press, 2017.

MLA Handbook for Writers of Research Papers, Modern Language Association of America, 2009.

Web Style Guide: Basic Design Principles for Creating Web Sites, 3rd ed., by Patrick J. Lynch and Sarah Horton, Yale University Press, 2009.

Vocabulary and words

New Oxford American Dictionary, 3rd ed., Oxford University Press, 2010.

Random House Word Menu, by Stephen Glazier, Random House, 1997.

Thesaurus of the Senses, by Linda Hart, Four Cats Publishing LLC, 2015.

Thesaurus.com, Roget's 21st Century Thesaurus, 3rd ed., Philip Lief Group, 2009.

Vocabulary for the College Bound Student, 4th ed., by Harold Levine, Perfection Learning, 2006.

Memory and mnemonics

How We Learn, The Surprising Truth About When, Where, and Why It Happens, reprint edition, by Benedict Carey, Random House Trade Paperbacks, 2015.

The Memory Book: The Classic Guide to Improving Your Memory at Work, at School, and at Play, illustrated edition, by Harry Lorayne and Jerry Lucas, Random House Publishing Group, 1996.

The Mind of a Mnemonist, a Little Book about a Vast Memory, revised edition, by A. R. Luria, Harvard University Press, 1987.

ACKNOWLEDGMENTS

Writing a grammar book is a form of teaching and, of course, learning. We thank the many teachers and students who generously contributed their time reviewing this book or offering tips and suggestions. We learned so much from their candid advice and support.

We sincerely appreciate and acknowledge the following reviewers for their invaluable feedback: Jill Broyles, Naomi Broyles, Noah Broyles, Sarah Broyles, Laurie Gessner, Mary Ann Hart, Bev Hughes, Ruth Ann Peck, Alexis Petrilla, Andrew Petrilla, Jim Petrilla, Madeline Petrilla, and Teresa Schleifer, editor extraordinaire. You all are the cat's meow.

We thank our supportive friends and family who kept us going through many book drafts and revisions. Special thanks to Grant Foreman, Ryan Foreman, Steve Foreman, Chris George, Kerry George, Kathleen Haney, Matt Haney, Michael Haney, Mary Ann Hart, Phillip Hart, Meghan Kolodziej, Julianne Lawler, Tommy Lawler, Carrie Ann Leib, Rayce Leib, Alexis Petrilla, Andrew Petrilla, Chuck Petrilla, Jason Petrilla, Jennifer Petrilla, Jim Petrilla, JoAnn Petrilla, and Madeline Petrilla for their love, encouragement, and suggestions.

Finally, we acknowledge the daily inspiration, joy, and comic relief we received from our cats Chloe, Susie, Tashi, and Tangi.

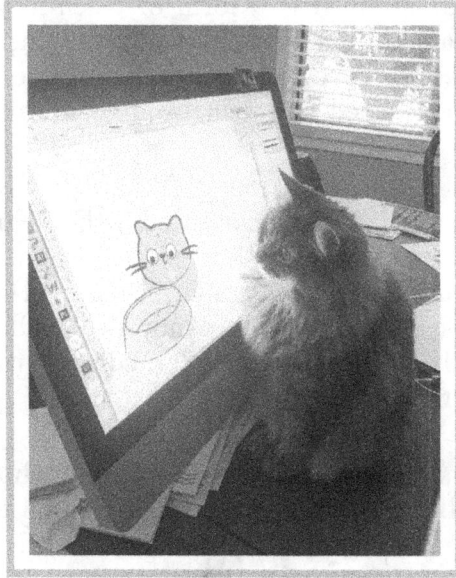

Chief cat advisor, Chloe,
oversees illustrations for
Cat Grammar Guide.

ABOUT THE AUTHORS

LINDA HART is a technical editor, writer, word and thesaurus collector, pollinator gardener, and native of Ohio. A graduate of University of Wisconsin, Linda has a bachelor's degree in chemistry and master's degrees in biochemistry, library science, and journalism. She is the author of *Thesaurus of the Senses*.

DON HART is a fiction and nonfiction writer, native of Ohio, and graduate of The Ohio State University. He was a mnemonics (memory) instructor for Osher Lifelong Learning Institute at University of Dayton for more than 25 years. He has taught in-service courses for teachers, college-level courses, and adult school classes at Clark State College, University of Dayton, and Sinclair College through Kettering Adult School. He has also taught grammar and writing to his homeschooled grandsons. Don is the co-editor and a contributing author of two short story collections: *Anthology of Christmas Memories* and *Anthology of Tragedies & Triumphs*.

CAT GRAMMAR SONG

If your spelling is a fright
And your commas aren't right
You need *Cat Grammar*.

If your writing's gone flat,
Then take it from a cat
Go read *Cat Grammar*.

Cat Grammar
When you're starting to stammer

Cat Grammar
Give your writing some glamour.

Cat Grammar
Cat Grammar
Cat Grammar

INDEX